COLVMBANVS

IN HIS OWN WORDS

TOMÁS Ó FIAICH

D1343049

VERITAS

First published 1974
Reissued 1992
This edition published 2012 by
Veritas Publications
7–8 Lower Abbey Street
Dublin 1, Ireland
publications@veritas.ie
www.veritas.ie

ISBN 978 1 84730 357 8

Copyright © Cardinal Tomás Ó Fiaich, 1974, 2012

10 9 8 7 6 5 4 3 2

A catalogue record for this book is available from the British Library.

Designed by Barbara Croatto, Veritas
Printed in the Republic of Ireland by Turner's Printing Limited, Longford

Veritas books are printed on paper made from the wood pulp of
managed forests. For every tree felled, at least one tree is planted,
thereby renewing natural resources.

Contents

Introduction

St Columbanus is a man of firsts in Irish history. The first Irish writer to leave a literary corpus, he is the first Irishman in the surviving literature to describe himself as Irish and to give an account of Irish identity.

Born in Leinster, he rose to prominence as master in the great monastery of Bangor on the shores of Belfast Lough until, secure and middle-aged, he left Ireland forever circa 591 in the company of a handful of followers and journeyed to continental Europe. There, with royal backing, he established a succession of monasteries: Annegray, Fontaine, and Luxeuil in the Vosges mountains, and Bobbio near Genoa. In time, Luxeuil and Bobbio grew to become major spiritual and cultural centres and produced some of the leading figures of continental Christianity. Guided by the Rules he wrote for monks, the monasteries became models for later foundations and, with their alumni, perpetuated Columbanus's monastic ideals long after his death in 615.

Columbanus's forceful personality is revealed in his writings – his Rules, sermons, and especially his letters to popes and to his followers – with their characteristic combination of profound spirituality and forthright adherence to principle. The letter he wrote to his followers as he waited to be sent back to Ireland following a conflict with the family of King Theuderich has an emotional charge that resonates down the centuries: 'So my speech has been outwardly made smooth, and grief is shut up within. See, the tears flow, but it is better to check the fountain; for it is no part of a brave soldier to lament in battle.' On the other hand, he was direct and unambiguous in his call to action when those in authority failed to use their power to give good leadership. From the supreme pastor of the Church he expected the supreme example of principled leadership. When it was lacking, it was his duty to confront the delinquent. To Pope Boniface IV, who reigned in the aftermath of the disastrous pontificate of Pope Vigilius, his demand for action was conveyed with characteristic and highly effective wordplay: 'Be vigilant, I beg you Pope, be vigilant, and again I say, be vigilant; since perhaps Vigilius was not very vigilant.' Considering his achievements and the example of sanctity that is his legacy, it is not surprising that Jonas of Bobbio's *Life of St Columbanus* should have appeared less than a generation after the saint's death. This is another first: Columbanus is the first Irishman to be the subject of a biography.

Many scholars have discerned a truculence, if not arrogance, in Columbanus's works. For them, he is a brash and abrasive old Irishman. However, in many cases his direct manner of speaking has obscured for a modern readership the subtlety of his theology and the spiritual depth of his arguments which are founded on biblical learning and the writings of the Church Fathers. He adapted that learning to find solutions to the problems that he and his Church faced. The causes of poor leadership – especially spiritual – that he diagnoses in his letters and sermons are as relevant now as when he wrote almost one-and-a-half millennia ago. Leadership, for Columbanus, is a matter of service to others, not a quest to fulfil personal ambition. Problems start when that order is reversed, that is, when leaders fail to act selflessly in exercising their power to guide those over whom they have been given authority, but instead see power as an opportunity for personal or institutional advancement and enrichment. The pastor who sets the material or reputational standing of his institution above the spiritual well-being of his flock is courting disaster. The worldly cleric cannot warn or reprimand the wayward, especially if the offender is powerful, for he is vulnerable to any threat to his wealth and reputation, or to the wealth and reputation of his Church. It is precisely for this reason that Columbanus believes that monks make the best spiritual guides. Detached from the world, they are unassailable. They cannot be pressured by threatening their wealth or family; they have none. They are immune even to threats to their lives for, writes Columbanus in his letter to the Gaulish, or French, bishops, they follow the good shepherd (John 10) who laid down his life for his sheep. Columbanus's analogy is pointed for the implication is that bishops are too concerned with material things and, therefore, their leadership is defective. As an example of their failure to cut their ties to the world, Columbanus mentions at the end of his letter to Pope Gregory the Great that he has heard their confessions and knows that, even after they entered the clerical state, they continue to sleep with their wives.

Shrines, towns and landmarks across Europe bear Columbanus's name and testify to the widespread diffusion of devotion to the saint. Indeed, he wrote with an awareness not just of an Irish identity, but in some sense as a European. In Columbanus's letter to Pope Boniface, Benedict XVI recently noted that 'we find for the first time the expression *totius Europae* ('of all Europe') with reference to the presence of the Church in the Continent'. Columbanus ends his letter to the Gaulish clerics on this theme of the unity of the European

Church reminding his readers that in the Church, national allegiance and racial identity have been superseded (but not replaced) by a spiritual identity, 'for we are all joint members of one body, whether Franks or Britons or Irish or whatever our races be'. This is more than a rhetorical flourish. Columbanus appeals here to the ancient image of the Church as a body. In a body, the individual members are bound together, their coordinated actions guided by concern for the good of the whole. In the body of the Church, the virtue that binds the members is *caritas*, 'charity'. Members must not act out of self-interest, but be mindful of the needs of others. The divisions that convulsed the Church in Columbanus's day, therefore, were seen as a grave threat. They indicated that the bonds of charity, the very foundation of the Christian community, had been ruptured. Christians had departed from the unity and charity of the Church of the apostolic age, that is, the Church as founded by Christ. Columbanus writes that loyalty to its past was essential if the Church was to regain its unity, and be fit to proclaim its message. On the other hand, to forget the past is the ultimate betrayal, it is an act of self-betrayal, a denial of one's origins and the loss of identity.

Columbanus's impact had a long afterlife, and was responsible ultimately for Ireland's reputation as the land of saints and scholars. He wrote of Ireland's location in 'the Western regions of the earth's farther strand' and used dramatic imagery to portray the coming of Christianity to his homeland. Christianity, like the sun, rose in the East. Just as the sun's journey across the sky is completed when it reaches Ireland, the last footfall in the West, so too the conversion of the Irish marked the point at which the Church fulfilled its mission to spread salvation to all peoples. In the middle of the ninth century, the biographer of St Gall, Columbanus's follower, acknowledges the debt of his people to Ireland 'whence the splendour of such light came to us'. The light of Christianity had shone westwards to Ireland, but now this light shines in the opposite direction, for the Irish led by Columbanus are the evangelisers, and those in eastern parts receive the light of salvation from the West. In that sense, this later tradition is a reflection of Columbanus's belief that the conversion of his homeland on the edge of the world led to the spiritual and cultural enrichment of the West.

In gathering selections from the works and Jonas's Life of Columbanus together in the original 1974 publication, Cardinal Tomás Ó Fiaich performed an important service by making that literature accessible to a wide readership, informing them of their own cultural and historical roots. This timely and unchanged reprinting of Tomás Ó Fiaich's anthology brings the words of Columbanus to a new generation.

Further reading
The essays in M. Lapidge (ed.), *Columbanus: Studies on the Latin writings* (Woodbridge, 1997) are the most recent and authoritative assessments of the works attributed to St Columbanus. For an account of his career, see T. M. Charles-Edwards, *Early Christian Ireland* (Cambridge, 2000), 344–90. For a treatment of his ideals of spiritual authority, see D. Bracken, 'Authority and duty: Columbanus and the primacy of Rome', *Peritia* 16 (2002), 168–213.

Dr Damian Bracken
School of History, University College Cork
15 February 2012

PART I

LIFE

I.
†HE MAN BEHIND †HE PEN

WHO COULD LISTEN TO A GREENHORN? WHO WOULD NOT SAY
AT ONCE: WHO IS THIS BUMPTIOUS BABBLER THAT DARES TO
WRITE SUCH THINGS UNBIDDEN?

st COLUMBAN, 5th LETTER

Jonas of Susa entered the monastery of Bobbio in 618. It was
a young monastery, founded only about five years earlier. Its
founder, Columban, had died three years before Jonas's arrival,
and was already becoming a legendary figure in the conversation
of those who had known him. An ideal situation, one would
think, for Jonas, the man destined to write Columban's life.

Jonas was born in the town of Susa, a pleasant place in the
Piedmontese Alps, only seven or eight miles from the present
French frontier. Even today, after nearly two thousand years,
its Roman remains are well preserved. In Susa itself and later
in Bobbio, Jonas studied Livy and Virgil in surroundings
which must have brought them easily to life again. He read
some of the pioneer efforts of Latin hagiography – the life
of St Martin of Tours by Sulpicius Severus, of St Hilary of
Poitiers by Fortunatus, of St Ambrose by Paulinus of Milan.
It was probably these which first gave him the idea of trying
to set down in similar form the life of Bobbio's founder,
Columban – that and the young writer's consciousness that he
and Columban were in a sense namesakes. For Jonas was the
Hebrew of the Latin *columba*, the dove.

Columban's successor as Abbot of Bobbio, Attala, who made Jonas his minister or secretary, was able to give him much first-hand information. So also were many of the other monks who had followed Columban from Luxeuil or joined him in Bobbio in his declining years. There was Bertulf, the third abbot of Bobbio, a native of Gaul, who had earlier been a monk in Luxeuil. Jonas accompanied him as his secretary to Rome in 628 to consult with Pope Honorius concerning the problems facing Bobbio. Next he was off to Luxeuil where Abbot Eustasius, one of Columban's favourite disciples, whom the Irishman was very happy to see as his successor there before his own death, was still happily reigning. Before or after his visit to Luxeuil Jonas had made the long journey across the Alps almost to the shore of Lake Constance where Gall, in his hermit's cell at the spot which still bears his name, recalled his years with Columban until the day when the two Irishmen disagreed.

By the end of the 630s Jonas was back in Bobbio. He had travelled much, met those best qualified to talk of Columban, seen the spread of monasticism throughout Gaul by men trained in Luxeuil. He was the obvious man to write Columban's story. Abbot Bertulf and the community urged him to write it but another task called him away for three years. We do not know its precise nature but it brought him first of all to the modern Belgium where Amand, the Bishop of that region, used him in the work of evangelisation. From Belgium he came into north-eastern France where by a lucky break he met three members of the one noble family who looked back to Columban as their father in God. Chagnoald was Bishop of Laon and had earlier been one of Columban's community in Luxeuil. Faro was now Bishop of Meaux, where his family had welcomed Columban after his expulsion from Luxeuil. Their sister Fara, dedicated to God by Columban in childhood, was now Abbess of Evoriacum, one day to be known as Faremoutiers in her honour and to become famous as a school for the daughters of kings and princes. Here Jonas began to put in order all the reminiscences of Columban that had been gathered over the years. It may have been 640 or 641 or even 642. There were new abbots in Luxeuil and Bobbio since he had last visited them and it was to these that Jonas addressed the carefully constructed preface of his work:

> To the Fathers Waldebert and Bobolenus, most distinguished masters, highly honoured in holy rule, strong in virtues of religion, Jonas a sinner: I remember that three years ago when I was staying in Bobbio during my wandering in the country of the Apennines I promised at the request of the brethren and on the order of Abbot Bertulf to write an account of the life and work of our beloved father Columban, particularly as so many of those who had lived with him and seen his work were still alive ...

He apologises for his lack of eloquence and clumsiness of expression and draws a series of ironical comparisons between his own poor efforts and the eloquence of scholars:

> They, drenched with the dews of eloquence, have adorned the green fields with flowers; for us the parched earth will scarcely produce a shrubbery. They are rich in the balsam of Engaddi and the perfumes of Arabia; for us butter from Ireland provides poor fare ... They seek the very exotic fruits of the palm tree; for us, as the poet of Italy (Virgil) has put it, the mild fruit of the humble chestnut ...

15

It was all a literary device, for Jonas had no need to be so apologetic about his shortcomings. He was a man of his age and of his environment, and like all hagiographers of those centuries he wished to edify his readers. The miraculous powers of his hero were emphasised; his shortcomings were glossed over or omitted. But within this framework he put his material into a consecutive narrative, mentioning people and places with a frequency which contrasts with Patrick's single *Silva Focluti*.

For all its faults, the life of Columban by Jonas lies behind everything that has been written about Columban by all the scholars ever since.

II.

An island monk

ALL WE IRISH, INHABITANTS OF THE WORLD'S EDGE, ARE
DISCIPLES OF SAINT PETER AND PAUL.

St Columban, 5th Letter

The middle of the sixth century was the period when the young
men of Ireland were frantically enthusiastic about becoming
monks. Just as they flocked in droves to the continental centres
of learning in the ninth century, to the new religious orders
in the twelfth and thirteenth centuries, to the Spanish and
French armies in the seventeenth and eighteenth centuries, to
the Irish Volunteers in 1913/14, the desire to take the monastic
habit and ultimately to found a new monastic house was the
ambition of a multitude around 550. For youths of spirit and
dedication it was the noblest call to be heard in the Ireland
of that era, combining practical Christianity, heroism, self-
discipline, initiative and sacrifice to give a new sense of purpose
to their lives.

Enda's foundation on the Aran Islands, drawing some of its
inspiration from Scotland, was the first motherhouse for these
young men on Irish soil and it sent out Finnian to Moville,
Eugene to Ardstraw, Tighearnach to Clones. Another Finnian,
this time of Clonard, who borrowed some of his ideas from
the Welsh monastic founders and reformers, became 'teacher
of the saints of Ireland' and sent out the next great group of
pioneers who have been given the picturesque title of 'the twelve

apostles of Ireland' – Columba to Derry (546), Durrow (556), and Iona (563), Ciarán to Clonmacnois (about 550), Brendan to Clonfert (554 or 559), Molaise to Devenish, Cainneach to Aghaboe, Mobhi to Glasnevin, Colman to Terryglass, Sinell to Cleenish. A third group of sixth-century foundations owed little or nothing to Clonard – Bangor, founded by Comgall (d.603), Moville on Strangford Lough founded by Finnian (d.579), Glendalough founded by Kevin (d.618), Tuam by Jarlath, Cork by Bairre. And a fourth group was founded primarily by and for women – Kildare by Brigid and Killeavy by Moninne before the end of the fifth century, Killeady in Co. Limerick by Ita, and Clonbroney in Co. Longford by Samhthann, in the sixth century.

Young men must have compared the rugged grandeur of Clonenagh with the emotional appeal of Clonmacnois. For the sixth-century Irish monastic founders also had their own contrasting styles – Columba the gentle scribe, Ciarán the craftsman, Brendan the boatman, Fintan the extremist in matters of mortification, Molua the companion of the animals and birds.

When the youthful Columban decided on further studies about 560 with a view to entering the monastic life, he opted for the monastery of Cleenish on Lough Erne. It had been founded only a few years before by Sinell, who had done his apprenticeship with Finnian at Clonard. But then nearly every monastery in Ireland around 560 had to be a young monastery. The Clonard tradition, passed on no doubt to Cleenish, placed great emphasis on study and intellectual formation. Jonas probably heard of this emphasis later, for he records that Sinell was 'famous for his holiness and for his learning in sacred things'.

Why had Columban to go so far from home to find a monastery to his liking? It has been conjectured that he was born about 543 on the borders of the modern counties of Carlow and Wexford. Jonas heard how the child's mother had dreamt before he was born that a brilliant sun arose from her breast and illuminated the whole world. In his youth he must have sat at the feet of a learned teacher, for Jonas records that he studied grammar, rhetoric, geometry and the Sacred Scriptures, all of which formed part of the curriculum of the Irish monastic schools.

As he grew to manhood he was good-looking and girls were attracted to him. His *formae elegantia*, as Jonas calls it, appealed particularly to one young woman who tried to ensnare him. Columban fought the temptation with the gospel as his shield and sought the advice of an anchoress who lived in a nearby cell. Jonas purports to reproduce the answer she gave him, but reading between the lines we get the impression that the biographer is here using a literary device – much as a later Gaelic writer might take off on an alliterative run in such a dramatic situation:

Fifteen years ago I abandoned my father's house to fight against temptation and sin. Christ is my leader. Since then the grace of God has kept me from turning back and if I were not a weak woman I would have crossed the seas in search of a wider battlefield. But you, burning with the fire of youth, stay at home. Whether you like it or not, you will find yourself in your weakness listening to the tempter's voice. Do you think you can go freely in the company of women? Don't you recall that Adam fell through the blandishments of Eve, that Samson was seduced by Delilah, that David fell through the beauty of Bethshabee, that the most wise Soloman was deceived through love of woman. Away with you, young man, go away from the destruction which has ruined so many, turn from the road that leads to the gates of Hell ...

Columban returned home for the last time, frightened but determined. He must break with the family circle for ever and dedicate himself completely to preparation for the life of self-sacrifice that lay ahead. He told his mother he was leaving home. She pleaded with him, burst into tears and threw herself across the threshold to block his exit. He asked her not to grieve, and then in the first of several decisions, which to our way of thinking seem so hard and unrelenting, decisions which often appear cruel and hurtful to his friends, he stepped across her prostrate body and set off for the north, knowing they would never meet again. Jonas puts into his mouth at this moment the hard words of St Jerome:

The enemy holds the sword over me to strike me down; so what should I care for a mother's tears ... The true piety here is to be cruel.

Under Sinell in Cleenish Columban laid the foundations of his future learning. His commentary on the Psalms and some of his poetry were written while he was still a young man – some of them may have been composed while in Cleenish but they seem to fit most easily into his long years in Bangor. We do not know how long Columban remained in Cleenish, but Jonas tells us that as soon as he decided to become a monk he entered the monastery of Bangor.

Comgall, the founder of Bangor, was one of the great monastic fathers of sixth-century Ireland. He had served his own apprenticeship under Fintan of Clonenagh in Laois, the father of the most austere tradition within Irish monasticism.

As the glossator of the *Martyrology of Oengus* put it:

Fintan fial,
níro tomhail re ré riamh,
acht arán eorna foeda
is uisce creda criad.

Generous Fintan
consumed nothing during his life-time
except bread of withered barley
and muddy water from the clay.

It was Fintan's stern discipline, tempered by the personal stamp of Comgall himself, that had become the Rule of Bangor.

We must not imagine Bangor – or indeed any of the great Irish monasteries of the sixth century, for Bangor was one of the greatest – like an earlier version of one of the great medieval monasteries on the Continent. It was much closer in appearance to the primitive monastic settlements of the Nile valley than to a later Monte Cassino or Clairvaux, a collection of round wooden huts built around a small church and surrounded by an embankment. When the Latin word *monasterium* was borrowed into Irish, it first gave the form *muintir* which was applied not to the monastic buildings but to the people who dwelt in them. In short, for the Irish the monastery was the community, not the buildings. In physical layout probably the closest approximation on Irish soil today to an early Irish monastery is Butlin's holiday-camp in Mosney, with its rows of small wooden chalets for sleeping in, grouped around a few larger communal buildings like the chapel and the dining hall.

From Adamnan's *Life of Columba*, written at the end of the seventh century by an author who explicitly mentions that he had talked with men who had become monks in the previous century, we can reconstruct an authentic picture of a sixth-century Irish monastery in great detail. The monks lived in small cells constructed of wood or wattles – Columban's own Rule later was to refer to a monk's *cellae suae cohabitator*, thus implying that two or more might share the same cell. Side by side with the living quarters of the monks within the enclosure were the communal buildings, i.e. church, refectory and guesthouse. Originally these were built of wood also. St Bernard described the later oratory of Bangor as made 'of smoothed planks closely and strongly fastened together'.

At the head of the monastic community stood the abbot, in some monasteries always chosen from the same family group. He was assisted by a kind of private secretary called the *minister* – in Bangor a certain Crimhthann acted as a *minister* for Comgall. A group of the senior monks – the *seniores* – were associated with the abbot in the direction of the community and the training of novices and from their ranks all offices of authority in the monastery were normally filled. The *oeconomus* was an important official who looked after the material resources of the monastery; other monastic office-holders, mentioned by Adamnan or Jonas, include the *scriba*, the guest master, and the cook or cellarer.

The daily fare of Comgall's monks was bread, vegetables and water; milk and milk products were permitted later when the founder's ultra-severe regime, inherited from Fintan of Clonenagh, was relaxed. As in other Irish monasteries the inmates wore sandals and a long white tunic covered by a coarse woollen outer garment and hood. Their daily life was a constant round of prayer, manual labour, study and mortification. They assembled in the church often each day for the recitation of the canonical hours, the night office being the most prolonged. They engaged in all the usual agricultural pursuits from the sowing to the threshing of the grain, and made the monastery self-sufficient not only in food but in drink, clothing, buildings and all kinds of implements and utensils. If Columban's own learning can be taken as an indication of the studies pursued in Bangor, the monks there attained a high standard of Latin learning and a smattering of Greek, read the pagan classical authors and were deeply versed in the scriptures. No doubt those monks who showed sufficient talent spent much time copying manuscripts but the earliest Bangor manuscript now preserved – the Antiphonary – dates from a century after Columban's departure. Fasting, silence, curtailment of sleep, repeated genuflections, prayer for prolonged periods with arms outstretched and corporal punishment inflicted on the palm with a leather strap were normal forms of mortification or could be imposed for breaches of Rule. It was a severe Rule, one of the hardest in any Irish monastery, yet for the seventh-century Bangor scribe it was:

> The good Rule of Bangor,
> Upright, divine,
> Diligent, holy and strict,
> Wonderful, just and sublime …

In this ascetic yet happy milieu Columban spent many years of his young manhood. He was chosen by the *seniores* to be raised to the priesthood and become one of the few ordained monks among a majority of lay religious. Although Jonas does not mention the fact, there is some evidence that he was placed in charge of Bangor's monastic school and it is mentioned in the

Lives of Gall and Deicola. When such an important figure in the monastic community first talked to Comgall of his desire to go abroad, he was rebuked by the abbot. But Columban finally convinced his superior that the call came from on high and Comgall gave his consent. Furthermore he allowed twelve of the brethren to accompany Columban on the great adventure. From references to some of the group by names in Jonas and in Columban's own letters, we obtain the names of most of them – Gall, the most famous after his master, Domoal, who acted as Columban's minister, Comininus, Eunocus, Equonanus and Columban óg (who died in Luxeuil), Libranus and Aedh, the member of the party in episcopal orders. Deicola and Lua were probably also in the original group and if it included Leobard and Caldwald they must have been the only two Anglo-Saxons among the twelve. The sea bore no terrors for such men – it was just outside the monastic enclosure at Bangor – and fortified by the blessing of Comgall they rowed courageously into the unknown. From this on, it was for Columban to take decisions on his own.

III.

WHITE BURGUNDY – AND RED

I BESEECH YOU BY OUR COMMON LORD ...
THAT I MAY BE ALLOWED WITH YOUR PEACE AND CHARITY TO
ENJOY THE SILENCE OF THESE WOODS AND TO LIVE BESIDE THE
BONES OF OUR SEVENTEEN DEAD BRETHREN, EVEN AS UP TILL
NOW WE HAVE BEEN ALLOWED TO LIVE TWELVE YEARS AMONG
YOU.

St COLUMBAN, 2nd LETTER

The voyage from Ireland was short and simple, says Jonas, though scholars have constantly disputed whether it brought Columban and his companions to Britain or Brittany. It seems most certain that they would have landed in Britain first just as other missionaries like Fursa and Feuillen did, proceeding to the continent later. Near Newquay harbour in Cornwall a place of ancient origin still bears the name of St Colomb. Perhaps it would not be too daring to suggest that the voyagers first sojourned there.

Across the Channel from St Colomb is the Bay of St Malo. It was near here, according to tradition, that our saint first set foot in Gaul. The village of Cancale is about six miles east of St Malo, and a granite cross here, still called after St Columban, bears witness to his travels in these parts. Once he arrived at Rouen he could join the Roman road going east, of which a branch led to Rheims, the 'capital' of the kingdom of the Franks.

In Columban's time the greater part of Gaul was ruled by the Merovingian dynasty of Frankish kings who descended from Clovis (d.511), their first Christian ancestor. Neustria comprised the territory lying roughly between the Loire and the Meuse; Austrasia the territory east of this as far as the Rhine and beyond it, continuing up the basin of the Rhine into Switzerland; Burgundy the territory south of this as far as the Rhone valley. For a generation, the three kingdoms had been convulsed by a series of bloody feuds and family murders which make up the darkest pages of Gregory of Tours. Of the grandsons of Clovis, only one, Gunthram, King of Burgundy and Austrasia, was still alive when Columban reached Gaul.

Jonas gives us only a very fleeting glimpse of Columban's early preaching in Gaul. In a land of spiritual desolation, still nominally Christian but where, due to war and negligent bishops, the practice of religion had collapsed, Columban and his companions were untiring, humble, patient. Did they use Latin or had they by this time picked up a smattering of one of the Germanic dialects which the Frankish rulers spoke? Gall became renowned later for his ability to learn languages, and perhaps the Latin-German vocabulary in Irish script which still remains in the Library of St Gallen and which, tradition says, was composed by Gall himself may have been Columban's *Teach Yourself German*. It contains words relating to the human body, the seasons and the weather, to farming and building, plants and animals, to travel by land and water. At any rate, the fame of his preaching reached the king and he was invited to visit the court.

Jonas calls the king Sigebert. But Sigebert had been dead since 575. Hence, just as scholars have argued about the year that Patrick reached Ireland, they have had to face the problem of the chronology of Columban. In this biography we have accepted 590/591 as the year of Coumban's arrival in Gaul, hence the king of Austrasia and Burgundy who received Columban at Rheims can only have been Gunthram. But it is only fair to add that some modern biographers place Columban's arrival in Gaul shortly after 570 when Sigebert was still reigning. This chronology avoids a clash with Jonas but gives rise to other difficulties.

Columban and his companions were well received by the king, who begged them to remain in his kingdom and promised them whatever they should ask. Columban replied that they wished only to follow the teaching of the Gospel: 'If any man will come after me, let him deny himself, take up his cross and follow me ...' The king's next offer was too attractive to be refused: 'If you wish to take up the cross of Christ and follow him, look for a more secluded place of retreat, but do not leave our territory nor pass to neighbouring peoples, so that at the same time you will increase your own reward and give us the chance of salvation.'

Columban and his twelve set out to explore the mountainous region of the Vosges. In the heart of the forests that straddled the vaguely defined border between Austrasia and Burgundy they came on the remains of an old Roman fort called Anagrates. It had been occupied since Attila and his Huns had blotted out Roman civilisation in these parts over a century earlier. Here in the valley of the Breuchin, surrounded by the wild beasts of the forest, they decided to make their home. In modern French it is the village of Annegray.

They repaired a ruined temple of Diana to serve as a church they dedicated to St Martin of Tours. After a triduum of prayer and fasting Columban marked out the monastic precinct and an enclosing trench was gradually dug to cut the monks off from the world. They cleared part of the forest and used the timber to build their cells. Jonas tells how they survived with appropriately miraculous aid. For food they had nothing at first except herbs, roots and the bark of trees. No wonder that one of them became ill of a fever. For three days they prayed and fasted from all food for the sake of the sick man. On the third day he was restored to good health Then a stranger suddenly appeared before the enclosure, his horses laden with bread and vegetables. He explained that his wife was seriously ill and a sudden inspiration made him come to relieve the monks in their hunger. The community implored God's aid for the sick woman and she was restored to good health.

But the day came soon enough when this stock of provisions was once again exhausted. For nine days they prayed and starved on herbs and bark. And then Carantoc, Abbot of Saulcy, a day's journey away across the rough terrain, was instructed in a dream to send aid to the men in the wilderness. He ordered his cellarer, Marculf, to load the monastery carts and set off, and as there was no path through the woods the horses made their way of their own accord to Columban's door. On his return Marculf told everyone what happened. He became in effect Columban's first PRO, and crowds of pilgrims began to flock to Annegray.

Thus arose the problem which has always plagued those who have abandoned the world. The world they had fled from pursued them – even into the cloister. In the Irish monasteries it became the practice for some of the monks to withdraw from time to time from community life, and go 'into the desert' to some nearby cave or forest. Names like Dysart, Disert, Diarmada, Desertoghill, Desertmartin – even 'the Desert', beside Armagh – still recall what were once the haunts of solitaries who had withdrawn from the crowded monasteries to more secluded retreats. Columban too searched the forests around Annegray for a spot so secluded that no human distractions would interrupt his contemplation. Again Jonas signposts the search with miraculous happenings.

One day in the solitude of the woods Columban was reading the scriptures and meditating on whether it would be better for the hermit to be attacked by wild beasts or to fall into the hands of brigands. Suddenly he was surrounded by twelve wolves but he still reflected that wild beasts were preferable as they are without sin. He calmly recited the verse from the psalm: 'Come to my aid, O God, O Lord, make haste to help me,' and the wolves turned and wandered off. Next came a party of Suabian brigands but they too left him unhurt. Finally, he found, four hundred feet above the valley of the Breuchin, the hermitage that would be his *carcair*. It was a cave scooped out of the rock. In it a bear had his den. 'Leave this place, never to return,' he ordered the bear, and with absolute docility the animal obeyed. Here Columban used to retire on the eves of Sundays and feast-days to pray without interruption. His minister Domoal sometimes accompanied him to bring messages to and from the community. On one such occasion he complained about having to carry up water from the spring below in the valley. 'Son,' said Columban, 'make a hollow in the rock. Remember that the Lord drew water from the rock for the people of Israel ...' Columban prayed and Domoal struck the rock and water gushed forth, which, as Jonas records, *'usque in hodiernum diem manet ...'* It is now St Columban's holy well on the hill above Annegray.

The number of monks increased so rapidly that it soon became necessary to open a second house. Columban did not go far afield in his search for a suitable place. Eight miles west of Annegray, beside the River Breuchin, lay the ruins of a former Roman fort at Luxovium which had been devastated by Attila and the Huns in 451. Its thermal springs that had once provided water for the Roman baths lay stagnant among the overthrown pillars.

King Gunthram died in 593 but young Childebert II, under the watchful eyes of the Queen Mother, Brunhilde, ruled over Burgundy and Austrasia. Through the good offices of one of his courtiers (Chagneric) the king's permission was sought and obtained – Chagneric was later to send his son to be schooled by Columban's monks. A new monastery, Luxeuil, arose amid the ruins, destined soon to outstrip its elder sister in size and importance. With its church dedicated to St Peter (and probably consecrated by Bishop Aedh who had accompanied Columban from Ireland), its refectory and its guesthouse, Luxeuil was to win undying fame through the splendour of its monastic school. As the community of monks, scholars and penitents continued to increase, a third foundation was made at Fontaine, three miles north of Luxeuil.

The three houses were under the direct control of Columban himself and he seems to have made Luxeuil the mother-house of the group. According to Jonas, the community at Fontaine numbered sixty monks, and as Luxeuil was undoubtedly the largest of the three it may be assumed that the total in three houses came to over two hundred monks. In fact, the Life of St Valericus, who was a disciple of Columban, places the number at 220. The dozen or so Irish monks were therefore very much of a minority in the three communities, especially as we have no evidence that they were reinforced by further recruits from the homeland, as happened in the case of the Schottenklöster centuries later. Some of the remainder were the sons of Frankish nobles who had come to Columban for their education, such as Chagnoald, the son of Chagneric who had played an important part in the foundation of Luxeuil, Donatus whose father was Duke of Upper Burgundy, and Waldelenus, the latter's nephew. Others were birds of passage like the priest Winioc whose son was destined to become fourth abbot of Bobbio and one of the two men to whom Jonas dedicated his Life of Columban.

Columban's community, scattered in three centres, was now large enough to demand the guidance of a written Rule. The abbot drew up for them his *Regula Monachorum*, more a series of general principles of monasticism than a detailed structuring of the monk's daily life. Obedience was the corner-stone of the whole system and the details of the communal life could be left to the will of whoever was chosen to be abbot. The ideal of poverty and mortification was inculcated through constant fasting, broken only by one meal a day of poor quality and taken late in the afternoon; the spirit of recollection had to be nurtured by silence and lead to repeated prayers. Only in the seventh chapter were detailed regulations laid down and these concerned the daily recitation of the Divine Office. Previous monastic founders had differed in their arrangement of the canonical hours, and Columban would opt for an unchangeable core to which other parts would be added according to the season. At the third (terce – 9.00 a.m.), sixth (sext – midday) and ninth (none – 3:00 p.m.) hours of the day the monks would assemble in the church to recite three psalms with versicles, and these remained unchanged throughout the year. So did the twelve psalms at nightfall (Vespers – 6:00 p.m.) and midnight (Midnocht) but the 3:00 a.m. office varied with the time of the year, reaching its maximum of thirty-six psalms during the long winter nights from 1 November until 1 February, the traditional Irish winter *ó Shamhain go dtí an chéad lá d'Earrach is d'Fhaoilleacha*. Saturday and Sunday mornings demanded double time in the church in preparation for the Lord's Day and day of rest, so that during the winter months the community chanted the whole psalter, the Irish *trí chaoga*, within these two nights. In nothing were the monks so directed as in this daily chanting of the Divine Office. A cough, a laugh, a late arrival all had their own penalties, with the cook and porter given more leeway than the rest to allow for an unexpected guest.

Columban's *Regula Coenobialis* lists in rather disorderly fashion the punishments to be inflicted for breaches of the Rule. Punishment was usually inflicted with a leather strap on the palm of the hand – for coughing at the beginning of the psalm and spoiling the singing, six slaps; for celebrating Mass with untrimmed nails, six slaps; for forgetting to say the prayer before or after work, twelve slaps; for forgetting the Blessed Sacrament when hurrying out to work, twenty-five slaps; for dropping it in the field, fifty slaps; and so on. To our way of thinking some of the punishments may appear severe but in a community which had absolute commitment to the ideal of self-denial they were accepted without a murmur.

Perhaps the most interesting feature of the *Regula Coenobialis* is the emphasis which it places on personal confession of faults. Twice a day, before the evening meal and before retiring at night, and at other times if desired, the monk was bound by the Rule to confess his sins, both mortal and venial, and an appropriate penalty was laid down. It was by their imposition of penances after private confession of sins, in the tradition of the Irish Penitentials, that Columban and his monks, when they applied the system also to the laity, changes the whole discipline of the early Church.

For the penitents both lay and clerical who flocked to Luxeuil, Columban wrote his Penitential. Excerpts will be given later from the Penitential as from the two monastic

Rules; it will suffice here to note that, like all the great monastic founders from Basil to Finnian, Columban's cure for sin was the practice of the opposing virtue: 'The talkative is to be punished with silence, the restless with the practice of gentleness, the gluttonous with fasting, the sleepy with watching, the proud with imprisonment, the deserter with expulsion ...'

IV.

Controversies and Expulsion

I SHALL NOT TREMBLE NOR IN GOD'S CAUSE SHALL I FEAR THE
TONGUES OF MEN, WHO LIE MORE OFTEN THAN THEY SPEAK
THE TRUTH.

St Columban, 5th Letter

By his penitential discipline, as Walker points out, Columban infringed powers vested in the local bishops; by his unauthorised foundations and his independence of action he ignored the diocesan bishop's prerogative and perhaps even the canons of the Church; by his celebration of Easter according to the Irish calculation he left himself open to a charge of unorthodoxy. There was probably little love lost between himself and several of the local hierarchy in any case; the hunting prelates denounced by Gregory of Tours and the simoniacal prelates denounced by Gregory the Great must have felt his presence an embarrassment. When Augustine of Canterbury was passing through France on his way to England in 596, he must have heard from them of this awkward customer in their midst, for Augustine's companion Laurentius was later to mention Columban's name as an example of uncompromising nonconformity in his letter to the bishops and abbots of Ireland.

The Gaulish bishops were already preparing to make a public issue of the Easter question when Columban, in the year 600, took the bold course of appealing over their heads to Rome. It is unlikely that he went there in person – in fact he mentions in two of his letters that he is unable to go – but he wrote his famous letter to Pope Gregory the Great strongly defending the Irish way of calculating Easter and enquiring with a nice touch of sarcasm if it was lawful for him to communicate with bishops who were 'after buying orders for money or after a secret adultery as deacons'.

Gregory seems to have deputed Conon, Abbot of Lérins, as intermediary, but in 603 the newly appointed Bishop of Lyons summoned Columban to appear before the Council of Châlon-sur-Saône. The Irishman had already sent his arguments to Rome in three volumes and forwarded a summary to the Bishop, but he declined to attend the synod in person lest he should argue and be quarrelsome. However, he set down his thoughts on the controversy in a letter to the assembled bishops: he first thanks God, not without a hint of irony, that for his sake 'so many holy men have been assembled', and then he adds with deep sarcasm: 'would that you met more often.' He asks for peace and charity 'to enjoy the silence of these woods and to live beside the bones of our seventeen dead brethren' as he has lived for twelve years past. The conclusion of the letter is a splendid plea for charity towards all without distinction of race: 'Pray for us, as we also pray for you, wretched though we be, and do not count us estranged from you for we are members of one body, whether Gauls or Britons or Irish or whatever our race …'

Pope Gregory the Great died in 604 and Columban wrote to his successor even before he discovered the name of the new Pope. As Columban's letters go, this one is a comparatively short one – for brevity was never his strong point in his writings – and again he requests that he and his monks may be permitted to follow the custom of their own country in the celebration of Easter. As his main argument for this he invokes the Council of Constantinople (381) which decreed that churches set up amid pagan tribes should follow the customs they had received from their ancestors. 'It is agreed,' he points out – ignoring completely the Gaulish hierarchy – 'that we are in our native land.'

It is probable that the Easter controversy, on its own, would never have led to Columban's expulsion from Gaul. Many of the Gaulish bishops were, of course, notably cool towards him, though this is not true of the local ordinary, Nicetius of Besançon, but they would scarcely have taken strong action against him without the support of the state. In his *Recollections of an Irish Rebel,* John Devoy expresses the belief that the Fenians would have defeated the Government on its own or the bishops on their own but they had no hope against a combination of the two. Columban soon found himself opposed by a similar combination.

King Childebert, successor of Gunthram, had died in 595 and his two sons became kings of Austrasia and Burgundy. They were both children and their grandmother Brunhilde acted as regent on their behalf. Soon Gaul was plunged once more into civil strife and the turn of the century became one of the blackest decades in an era which had few bright spots. As Theuderich (*Fr* Thierry, *Germ* Dietrich), the young king of Burgundy, came to manhood, he installed a number of concubines in the royal household and soon had four illegitimate children.

Jonas depicts dramatically the saint's reaction to the young king's wayward life. He went to see Queen Brunhilde who led out the four royal bastards to meet him. Columban asked who the children were. 'They are the king's sons,' she answered, 'confirm them with your blessing.' It may be that Brunhilde's ulterior motive was to secure a seeming approbation in the presence of the courtiers for the young men who would one day press their claim to succeed their father. Whatever the reason Columban refused to be associated with the ruse. 'You must know,' he thundered, 'that these will never hold the royal sceptre because they were begotten in sin'; and then he stormed out of the palace. It was the beginning of the end for his mission in Gaul and in a sense he had brought it on himself. But knowing Columban's strong personality by this time we would have been surprised if his answer had been any other.

This event marked the beginning of the Queen Mother's active hostility. Orders were issued for a boycott of the Columban monasteries by the people of the surrounding countryside. Columban decided to appeal in person to the king, and Jonas delights in telling how the saint refused to enter the royal palace and smashed the goblets of wine and the bowls of food sent out by the king for his reception. Inspired by terror Theuderich and Brunhilde promised improvement. But Brunhilde continued behind the scenes to urge the need for an investigation into Columban's monasteries and in this she found plenty of support from the bishops, the courtiers, the vassels and ultimately from the king himself.

Finally Theuderich rode out with a company of his followers to confront Columban in Luxeuil. The king demanded to know why entry was not allowed to all into the more secluded parts of the monastery. Columban replied that outsiders were not allowed to enter the living quarters of the servants of God but that appropriate hospitality was provided for all such guests. The king demanded free entry for all to the whole monastic complex, 'if you wish to retain the gifts of our generosity and our full support ...'. Columban answered that any such violation of the cloister would mean the end of the monastery, and if Theuderich were responsible for this, Columban prophesised that it would soon be followed by 'the destruction of his kingdom and the scattering of his race'. Then the king announced his decision – those of the monastic community who wished to cut themselves off completely from all men must leave Burgundy and return to the place from which they came. Columban replied that he would not leave the monastic enclosure unless dragged by force.

The king made no attempt to seize him but rode away from the monastery, leaving the final act to be performed by Count Baudulf and his followers. And it was this minor feudal magnate who seized Columban by force and carried him 'into exile', as Jonas calls it, to Besançon. The abbot had only a few of his fellow Irishmen for company, including his faithful secretary Domoal.

During a long halt in Besançon, Columban was granted permission to preach to the condemned convicts in the city's jails, and having obtained a promise of repentance from them if they obtained their liberty, he ordered Domoal to set them free. Again Jonas clothes the story of their escape in miraculous details – their fetters collapsed at the touch of Domoal and the local church doors opened to receive them and remained closed against their pursuers. In Besançon too, Columban was hospitably received by the local bishop, Nicetius, and found shelter in his residence. But his heart still pined for his brethren in Luxeuil and one Sunday morning, hoping that Theuderich would not interfere again, he returned quietly to the silence of its cloister.

But Columban had not reckoned on the depth of Brunhilde's enmity. A week later she heard of his return and persuaded the king to send further emissaries to remove him. Columban was miraculously delivered from the hands of one such band, but finally the king sent his own chamberlain, Count Bertechar, with an armed expedition under its captain, Ragamund, to enforce his decision. The community was in the church chanting the office when they arrived in Luxeuil. Bertechar and his men tried to persuade Columban to obey the king's command as they would otherwise be forced to carry out what was for them a very unpleasant task. But the Irishman was unbending to the end: 'I left my native land for the love of Christ; I shall not leave this place unless I am forced to.' Then, ordering the community to continue the office after his departure where it had been interrupted, he raised his hand in blessing and gave himself up.

Bertechar's orders were that the Irish and Breton monks were to accompany their master but those born in Gaul were to remain in Burgundy. So with a small group of fellow Celts – Deicola and Lua and Eunoc, probably Aedh and certainly Gall – Columban placed himself under the control of the Captain Ragamund and his men. It was the year 610 AD, almost two decades since the foundation of Luxeuil.

In Jonas's narrative their progress across central France was marked by a series of remarkable and often miraculous happenings. Yet it must have been a very exhausting march for men who were no longer young. Columban himself was nearing seventy and Nantes was six hundred miles away. Only a few miles from Luxeuil one of Columban's Irish companions – Deicola (perhaps his Irish name was Dicuil or even Céile Dé) – gave up exhausted and having obtained his master's permission settled in that region to become founder of the great Abbey of Lure. His later *Vita* represents him as the brother of Gall. In Besançon Columban found time for a brief visit to Bishop Nicetius to whom he recommended his foundations in the Vosges. Then on through Autun and Saulieu to Avallon where

Columban was attacked with a lance by a horseman who was a victim of demonic possession until cured by the Irish saint. In fact Jonas records the cure of seventeen other cases of demonic possession on this stage of the journey, five near the spot where the famous pilgrimage church of Vézelay was later erected and twelve in the residence of Theodemanda along the Cure river just before it enters the Yonne. At Auxerre, where St Patrick may have received part of his training nearly two centuries earlier, Columban prophesied that Clothair, King of Neustria, who had just lost the town to Theuderich, would be master of all Burgundy in three years. At Nevers the company embarked by boat on the Loire, and when one of the soldiers attempted to hurry the old Irish monk, Lua, by striking him with an oar, he was upbraided by Columban who prophesied that divine vengeance would strike himself in turn on this spot. (On his return, says Jonas, he was drowned there.)

From Nevers they sailed to Orléans, where all churches were closed against them by order of the king and the Irishmen found it difficult to obtain food until a Syrian woman and her husband came to their rescue. At Tours, after his request for permission to land had been refused, Columban passed a night in prayer at the tomb of St Martin. When the local Bishop, Leoparius, invited him to dine, he had an exchange of words at table which is preserved verbatim by Jonas and again throws some further light on Columban's character. When the bishop asked him the cause of his return to his own country, Columban could suppress his resentment no longer: 'It is that dog Theuderich who has torn me from my brethren.' One of the guests who was in the service of Theuderich and was married to the king's aunt remonstrated with the Irishman: 'Is it not better,' he asked, echoing a well-known proverb, 'to drink milk rather than gall?' 'I see you intend to remain faithful to your master,' said Columban; 'I am glad of the opportunity to send him such an excellent messenger. Go tell him that within three years he and his sons will perish.'

The courtier was shocked: 'Is this the speech of a man of God?' he asked. 'Why do you use such words?' 'Because I cannot keep silent the words the Lord has given me to speak,' replied Columban.

Finally they reached Nantes near the mouth of the Loire. The local bishop, Soffronius, was hostile – in fact he was co-operating with the state authorities to hasten their departure, thus allowing Ragamund and his soldiers to depart before Columban would sail.

From Nantes Columban wrote what he thought would be his last letter on French soil to his sons in Luxeuil. It is a letter full of tenderness and resignation in which he attributes all his misfortunes to Satan. He urged his monks to avoid dissension and preserve unity at all costs. To this end he named Attala as his successor but asked him to get rid of troublemakers. If Attala wished to follow himself into exile, Waldelin should succeed him, or failing him, whomsoever the community would elect. He pointed out that he was being compelled by force to return to Ireland, yet he could escape, for even the guards seemed to wish it. He concluded by asking his sons in Burgundy to pray for him.

As the merchant vessel on which it was intended that he and his companions should sail for Ireland was preparing for her departure, Columban made an unusual request to the local ecclesiastical and civil authorities: 'Let all my companions and the baggage be put on board; I will take a small boat from the Loire as far as the open sea.' Was he trying perhaps to emulate those Irish monks who sailed off in an open boat without oars, leaving it to their Divine Master to guide them whither he wished them to go? At all events aid came from the heavens. While Columban was still waiting at the mouth of the river, a storm blew up which drove the ship around. For three days the captain failed to re-float his vessel; then, taking it as a sign that he was not to co-operate in the expulsion of the monks from Gaul, he put themselves and their belongings ashore, and friend and foe alike were convinced that God wished Columban to stay.

V.

Wanderer for Christ

I AM ALWAYS MOVING FROM THE DAY OF BIRTH UNTIL THE DAY
OF DEATH.

St Columban, 6th Sermon

Since Columban dared not return within the territory of
Theuderich, he headed north towards Soissons to the court
of Clothair II, King of Neustria, a first cousin of Theuderich's
father. Clothair received him kindly and even invited him to
found a monastery in Neustria, but Columban declined the
invitation. He was still at the court when emissaries arrived
from the two grandsons of Brunhilde, each seeking Clothair's
support against the other in the quarrel which had broken out
between them. 'Stay neutral,' advised Columban, 'and within
three years you will be master of their states and their crowns
will be yours' – the third time he made such a prophecy.

From Neustria, Columban and his companions headed
east towards Austrasia on the first stage of a journey which,
it would seem, Columban intended to end only in Rome. At
the gates of Paris he healed a man possessed by an evil spirit.
Not far from Meaux in the valley of the Marne, which another
Irishman, St Fiachra, would make his own in a few score
years, Columban rested with his former benefactor, Chagneric,
and blessed his little daughter of nine years, one day to be
foundress of Faremoutiers. Continuing up the valley of the
Marne, Columban was received by a rich landowner and his

wife, who asked a blessing for their children in return. Their names were to be renowned later – Ado, founder of the double monastery of Jouarre; Audoen, founder of Rebais, and Rado, chief benefactor or Reuil.

Finally Columban and his companions reached Metz, seat of the court of Austrasia, where they were well received by King Theudebert. But there were others to welcome him here also, men whom Columban thought in Nantes he would never see again. Hearing that their beloved founder was on his way to Metz, many of the Luxeuil community had come to join him there – Eustasius who had received the last fond farewell, and Attala who had succeeded as abbot but preferred the lowest place in Columban's company to the highest in Luxeuil without him. Chagnoald who brought news from his father Chagneric, Bobelin, Ursicinus and several others. A permanent place of residence for this large community was obviously needed once more.

King Theudebert invited the monks to settle in the eastern borderland of his kingdom where they could preach the Gospel to the pagan tribes. With all central Europe to pick from, Columban headed for Bregenz on the south-east shore of Lake Constance, but he indicated that when his task there was accomplished he would continue his journey to Rome.

The voyage from Metz to Bregenz was accomplished on one of the great waterways of the world. First they sailed down the winding Moselle as far as Koblenz, the confluence of that river and the Rhine. Then up the Rhine to Mainz along that world-famous (see map on p. 160 tracing Columban's journey throughout Europe) stretch which is nowadays regarded as the most beautiful part of this most romantic of rivers. Past vineyards and cliffs and rocky promontories, many of them to be crowned later by audaciously perched castles, whose ruins remain today. Past St Goar which would receive its name from a missionary from his own country. Past the Lorelei rock where the legendary maiden waited to coax her victims to disaster. Past Bingen where Judge Keogh of the 'Pope's Brass Band' was to meet his sordid end. And so, on to Mainz where Columban was succoured by the local bishop who found him at prayer in his church.

Jonas is silent about the arduous journey of the Irish monks up the Rhine towards the modern Swiss frontier. Their course brought them past the later imperial cities of Worms and Speyer. Yet we are not completely in the dark, for Columban's rowing-song composed on the Rhine refers to storms and squalls and the need for manly strength to carry on. At Basle, according to tradition, Ursicinus left the company and in the mountains of the Jura built for himself the hermitage which was to be the forerunner of the Abbey of St Ursanne. If he came from Ireland, his name may be merely a Latinisation of the Irish name Mathghamhain.

From the Rhine Columban and his followers turned aside into its tributary, the Aare, and then into the latter's tributary, the Limmat, as far as Lake Zurich. Along the lake shore they came to Tuggen where they decided to sojourn for a while. One reason was possibly that the local people were Celts. The Alemannic tribesmen in the neighbourhood, the only German tribe which had resisted Christianity, still worshipped Woden, and Columban made few converts among them. But the impulsiveness of Gall, who set fire to their temples and threw their offerings into the lake, spoiled his master's efforts. Learning of a plot to murder Gall, Columban decided to depart quickly, and the whole community was on the move once more.

On the southern shore of the Bodensee (Lake Constance) they found a Christian community in the old Roman town of Arbon. Its priest, Willimar, entertained them hospitably for a weekend and his three deacons made the acquaintance of Gall whom they were later to join in the evangelisation of this region. From Willimar, Columban learned more about the deserted Roman town of Brigantium at the south-eastern corner of the lake. In such an old fort he had started life at Annegray; it seemed the place to which God was directing him.

The fifteen-mile journey from Arbon to Bregenz was made in a small rowing boat across the lake. At the point where the Upper Rhine flows into the lake they disembarked and found a ruined chapel dedicated to St Aurelia which had been converted into a pagan temple. Its restoration to Christian worship was to be their first task.

According to Walafrid Strabo's ninth-century life of St Gall, the monks fell in love with the place. Jonas, on the other hand, heard that they did not like Bregenz. Once again the task of preaching to the Alemanni in their own language fell to Gall, for he had, as Walafrid Strabo puts it, 'no small knowledge of the barbaric speech'.

Walafrid gives a very vivid account of the direct confrontation between the Irish and the Alemanni in the church of St Aurelia at Bregenz. Gall first preached to the multitude and called on them to turn away from the worship of the bronze images which they had affixed to the walls of this former church. He then took down the images, broke them with stones and threw them into the lake. Some who revered the old gods departed in rage but others remained to worship Christ. Then Columban blessed water and sprinkled it around the building while the monks walked in procession around it, chanting psalms. Finally Columban proceeded to the altar which he anointed with oil, and having placed the relics of St Aurelia within it he put an altar-cloth upon it and celebrated Mass. The new Irish monastery had been set up at Bregenz, probably towards the end of 610.

It is to Walafrid Strabo rather than to Jonas that we must go for details of the Columban community at Bregenz during their short stay there. Walafrid says they stayed for three years but as their period stretched from the end of 610 to the beginning of 612 the exaggeration is understandable. The monks built a small cloistered monastery, laid out a garden and planted fruit trees. Gall, still the enthusiastic fisherman, wove nets, and reaped a rich harvest from the Rhine and the Bodensee. Life proceeded much as it had in Luxeuil and the biographers fill in the narrative with miraculous happenings of the same type which we have already met in Burgundy – for instance, how a neighbouring prelate, probably the Bishop of Constance, made a gift of wheat to the monks when they were in want and how Columban ordered a bear to leave part of the wood to himself so that he could pray there without distraction.

One story told by Jonas describes how Columban came on a crowd of pagans gathered in the woods around a vat of beer which they were offering to Woden. The saint breathed on the cauldron and it burst with a loud noise so that all the beer poured out on the ground. Jonas must have smiled as he added the comment of the astounded pagans that 'the man of God has great strength in his breath'.

Events such as this – and despite the later overlay of legend they probably had some basis in fact – scarcely endeared the Irishman to the neighbouring peoples, but as long as the monks enjoyed the protection of the King of Austrasia they were comparatively safe. However the three years' further reign which Columban had predicted for him was nearing its end. Although some modern biographers of the saint have questioned whether he could have made the long double journey from Bregenz to Metz and back again to interview King Theudebert, Jonas is quite definite about this visit. Columban begged the king to abdicate his throne and enter the monastic life. The monarch greeted this request with laughter which was echoed by his courtiers. 'Who,' they asked 'had ever heard of a Merovingian king becoming a cleric of his own free will?' But Columban had the last laugh as he replied: 'If he does not become a cleric of his own free will, he will shortly become one by force.'

In the spring of 612 the long-threatening war between Austrasia and Burgundy broke out at last. The Austrasian army was first defeated at Toul and then the two fratricidal brothers with their armies clashed on the battlefield of Tolbiac where their great-great-grandfather Clovis had founded the Christian kingdom of the Franks more than a century earlier. It is now the German town of Zulpich, nearly half-way between Aachen and Bonn. 'So close was the fight and so frightful the butchery,' wrote a chronicler, 'that the corpses of the slain had no room to fall but remained standing among the living fighters.' The Austrasian army under King Theudebert himself was annihilated and the king fled across the Rhine and was captured for his brother Theuderich by the same Count Bertechar who had expelled Columban from Luxeuil two years before. By order of the Queen Mother Brunhilde, Theudebert was tonsured and put in a monastery, only to be beheaded shortly after.

On the day of the battle, Columban, who was with Chagnoald in the forest near Bregenz, had a vision of the slaughter. 'Father,' exclaimed the young monk, 'pray for Theudebert that he may obtain the victory over Theuderich, our common enemy.' 'You give advice that is foolish and contrary to the Gospel,' replied Columban. 'The Lord asked us to pray for our enemies.'

The death of Theudebert meant that Columban's prosecutor (Theuderich) now added Austrasia and the German provinces which went along with it to his former kingdom of Burgundy. Brunhilde set up her court at Metz. Deprived of his protector and once more under the rule of the king and queen who had expelled him, Columban now had to face the wrath of the local pagans whom he had previously offended. Some of them had complained to Duke Gunzo that the monks were interfering with the hunting in his woods and the order came from him that they were to leave Bregenz. Columban made no attempt this time to try on his old intransigence, for two of his monks were murdered in the woods when they were searching for one of the monastic cows which had been stolen. Other monks recovered their bodies which were carried back to the cloister for burial.

Columban's first plan seems to have been to traverse the forests of the Algau and reach the Danube basin. A vision convinced him however that he should head for Italy and he announced his decision to the community. For some reason which is not clear to us now, this decision was not universally popular. Perhaps the monks of the various Germanic tribes had no wish to leave their own peoples and go into a strange country. Some, like Chagnoald and Eustasius, returned then or shortly afterwards to Luxeuil. Even among the few surviving Irish monks Columban's word no longer met with a universal response, for Gall, with his knowledge of the Germanic dialect, was reluctant to follow his master.

The circumstances in which Columban and Gall parted for ever in this life must have made that parting one of the greatest sorrows of Columban's life, yet Jonas is silent about it. One can only suppose that Gall was reluctant to discuss it during his meeting with Jonas or perhaps asked the biographer not to pass on to further generations what must have hurt him to the core. Hence we must have recourse here again to Walafrid Strabo who presumably gives it as it had come down in the monastery of St Gallen: 'When the time for their departure was at hand, Gall fell suddenly ill of a fever. He threw himself at the abbot's feet and said he was suffering from a severe illness and was unable for the journey. Columban said to him: "Brother, I know that now it seems a heavy burden to you to suffer fatigue for my sake. Nevertheless, this I enjoin on you before I go, that so long as I live in the body, you do not dare to celebrate Mass."'

The decision seems very hard to us today. Even Walafrid Strabo felt that some excuse had to be made for it, as he added that Columban thought Gall was held back by love for the place where he had worked and by fear of the fatigue of the long journey. Yet Columban was usually full of tenderness for his monks when they were ill. Not knowing the full circumstances of the incident we cannot presume to judge the rights and wrongs of a disagreement between saints. But it bears out once again that, faced with a hard decision which he believed to be his duty, Columban would let no personal ties stand in his way.

So the two parted, Gall to row back with his nets across the lake to Arbon, where the priest Willimar and his clerics nursed him back to health and then found him the place of retreat along the river Steinach that would one day bear his name; Columban to follow the road through the mountains from Bregenz to Chur.

We do not know how many monks were in his company and it is only by inference that we can record a few of their names. One was Attala who would one day become Abbot of Bobbio. Another was Sigebert, who left the party at Chur and found himself a hermitage near the foot of the St Gotthard which was to grow into the renowned abbey of Disentis. As far as we know Columban was the only Irishman in the group. South of Chur we lose sight of him altogether in the pages of Jonas and it is only by having recourse to church dedications and local traditions that, as will appear later, a particular route may be suggested as the one he probably followed.

Whatever pass he took through the Alps must have been a severe trial for a man of seventy, involving as it did an ascent to over seven thousand feet before the Plain of Lombardy began to appear in the distant south. When we catch up with him in Jonas he is already in Milan at the court of the Lombard king.

The Lombards, like the other races among whom he had spent his continental years, were a Germanic people, but they were Germans with a difference. For one thing they were the only Germanic people who had settled in what is now Italy – a colonisation which had taken place during Columban's own lifetime. For another, they had been converted not to the Roman form of Christianity but to the Arian one which did not acknowledge the divinity of Christ. Yet Columban and his monks were kindly received by King Agilulf and his Queen, the pious Theudelinda. As so often happened in the past the king invited the Irishman to remain in his territory and promised a site for a monastery wherever he would choose.

Columban remained in Milan for a considerable time in 613. To this period belongs his most successful poem. True to his nature he was soon plunged into the Arian controversy. Jonas tells us that he wrote a short learned work in flowery style against the heretics but no copy of it survives. It was probably in Milan also that he composed and delivered the series of sermons which are still preserved. In the first he emphasises the Catholic doctrine of the Trinity, the one most consistently attacked by the Arians.

From Milan also he addressed his remarkable letter to Pope Boniface IV (608–615). To comprehend fully the background to this letter would take us across a century and a half of controversy from the days of St Patrick, when Nestorians and Monophysites were condemned, down to the 'Three Chapters' controversy in the middle of the following century. This series of schisms and controversies had left utter confusion among the Lombard bishops and civil rulers. One group was in union with Rome, another had fallen into schism. No sooner had Columban crossed their frontier than he was warned by the Bishop of Como in a letter that Pope Boniface was suspected of Nestorianism. His reply is unfortunately not extant. At the Lombard court he heard the Pope attacked as a supporter of heretics and all his native loyalty to Rome welled up within him. When King Agilulf asked him to write to the Pope – and, it was said, promised to accept his decision if only the Pope would show where the truth lay amid all the arguments – Columban welcomed the task.

This is the longest surviving letter, running to five thousand words, and as Francis McManus points out 'would require about forty minutes to be read aloud at an intelligible pace'. He calls all kinds of literary devices to his aid: alliteration, assonance, metaphors – of the Church sailing on a stormy ocean and marching into battle with trumpets blaring – proverbs (for how could an Irishman resist the *seanfhocail* on such an occasion?), even puns. He returns to the worn-out pun on his own name and coins a much better one on the name of Pope Vigilius who had bowed to the condemnation of the 'Three Chapters' at the emperor's behest: *Vigilia itaque, quaeso, papa; vigila et iterum dico vigila, quia forte non bene vigilavit Vigilius*. Apart from the somewhat obsequious opening paragraph – and presumably this was demanded by the accepted standards of polite address at the time – the letter is written with sincerity, vigour and boldness almost to the point of aggressiveness.

We do not know if Pope Boniface replied or even if the letter reached him safely. But the fact remains that for want of definite direction from Rome, Agilulf remained an Arian till his death and the 'Three Chapters' controversy continued to disturb the Church for the best part of another century. Although a later story makes Columban visit Rome in person, it almost certainly has no basis in fact. Jonas, as we have seen, omitted several events of the saint's life; in fact he has nothing about the controversial letter to Pope Boniface. But a visit to the Pope – if it had taken place – would certainly not have been omitted by him.

VI.

REPOSE AT LAST

SINCE WE ARE TRAVELLERS AND PILGRIMS IN THE WORLD, LET
US EVER PONDER ON THE END OF THE ROAD, THAT IS OF OUR
LIFE, FOR THE END OF OUR ROADWAY IS OUR HOME.

St COLUMBAN, 8TH SERMON

While Columban was still in Milan, a native of Northern Italy named Jucundus called the attention of King Agilulf to the ruined church of St Peter in the hilly country nearly seventy miles to the south, where the Bobbio stream flows into the Trebbia on its way to join the Po. It was the sort of terrain after which the Irishman seemed to hanker – wild, well watered, wooded and remote. The king offered the site to Columban together with the land within a perimeter of four miles, and the Irishman accepted gladly. He was surely pleased to be moving once more from the affairs of kings and bishops to the solitude which he loved.

His journey took him through Lodi, Pavia and Piacenza and along the shallow valley of the Lambro where the town of San Columbano now stands. The many marks with which this area still reveres his memory will be treated in their proper place. In Bobbio his first task was to restore St Peter's Church and Jonas gives us striking glimpses – not without their miraculous overtones – of the seventy-year-old abbot out on the slopes of Monte Penice, helping to provide timber for its rebuilding. Before the winter of 614 set in, a new Irish monastery, Bobbio, had taken shape in the foothills of the Apennines. And some distance to the north-east and to the south-west of the monastery were the two secluded caves to which the abbot would return at times to be alone with God.

Back in Gaul, Columban was not forgotten. The victorious Theuderich of Burgundy had died at Metz in 613, only half a year after the murder of the defeated Theudebert. Queen Brunhilde was captured by the army of Neustria, and having been first flogged, stripped naked and exhibited on a camel's back for three days by order of King Clothair, she was then tied by the hair to the tail of a wild horse which galloped in different directions until it tore her body to pieces. Her body was then burnt like offal outside the camp. Jonas notes the triumph of King Clothair as the fulfilment of Columban's three prophecies.

The king himself, now master of nearly all Gaul, sent Abbot Eustasius of Luxeuil with an escort of noblemen all the way to Bobbio to invite Columban to return to Luxeuil. But Columban tactfully declined the invitation while exhorting Eustasius to be a good abbot and to seek the king's assistance for Luxeuil. In a letter to King Clothair, which has not survived, the Irishman issued some words of rebuke – perhaps taking him to task for the inhuman degradation offered to Queen Brunhilde. It is the last writing from his pen of which we have a definite record.

It is surprising that Jonas tells us so little about Columban's death. Presumably everything concerning it was too well-known to need a chronicler when he entered Bobbio as a novice three years later. If, as tradition holds, the saint died not in the monastery but in his mountainside retreat, this may also help to explain Jonas's lack of information. Yet the death of a saint offers possibilities to a hagiographer of the Jonas type which we was unwise to ignore. See how half a century later

Adamnan turned the death of St Columba of Iona into one of the most touching passages of Western hagiography.

In his last days on earth Columban's thoughts were on Gall, the last surviving Irishman of the gallant band who had accompanied him from Bangor, his constant companion over half the roads of Europe, still 'silenced' because his obedience had been less than 'unto death'. On his deathbed Columban ordered that the staff with which he trudged through the Vosges and the Jura, the Alps and the Apennines, should be sent to Gall as a token of forgiveness. Then in the early hours of Sunday, 23 November 615, he breathed his last.

Hundreds of miles to the north Gall roused his deacon Magnoald and told him to prepare everything necessary for the celebration of Mass. To the astonishment of the deacon he confided: 'I have learnt in a vision that my Lord and father Columban has passed from the miseries of this life to the joys of Paradise this day. Therefore I must offer Mass for his repose.' As soon as Mass was over Magnoald was despatched post-haste to Bobbio where he discovered that everything had happened just as Gall had seen in the vision. After a stay of one night he set out again on the eight-day journey to St Gallen, bearing a letter from the monks describing Columban's last hours, and, in addition, the staff of forgiveness. For more than a decade Gall treasured it, not only as his master's parting gift but more so as the sign that his three years of penance were at an end. Having turned down an invitation borne by six Irish monks to him to become Abbot of Luxeuil on Eustasius's death in 627, he remained in the Lake Constance area until his own death at Arbon. The year is not certain, perhaps around 630. He was buried near the altar of his former cloister. He must have been a lonely figure in his last decade, for all those who had left Ireland along with him were long since dead or far away in Luxeuil. Yet he had his consolation. Columban had seen his foundations placed in great peril by his own expulsion from them; Gall lived long enough to see them made permanent and produce fruit a hundredfold. Before his death much of Western Europe was dotted with monasteries founded by Columban's disciples.

VII.
THE STAMP OF GREATNESS

NOW I SHALL CLOSE MY LAST WORDS WITH A HUMBLE PRAYER:
BE YOURSELF MINDFUL OF ME WHEN YOU READ THESE VERSES.
ST COLUMBAN, VERSES TO SETHUS

One could write a whole volume on the character and personality of Columban – his austerity, forthrightness, courage, unworldliness. Yet how can these virtues and a score of others, many of them at first sight mutually contradictory, be summed up in a few paragraphs? In one of the finest passages in his edition of *Sancti Columbani Opera*, G.S.M. Walker has succeeded brilliantly in drawing these various strands together and the personality that emerges from them is a powerful figure who bears the stamp of greatness. In seeking to identify the salient features of Columban's personality, I feel that it would be presumptuous of me to try to improve on Walker's words:

> It is the misfortune of commanding characters to arouse consuming hatreds; and Columban, by the outspoken freedom of his language and the tenacious independence of his mind, was plunged into animated quarrels for the greater portion of his active life. His integrity was hard and cutting as a diamond. Ruthless to himself, he could be inexorable in his demands on others with a determination that not even a mother's tears were able to soften into

compromise. Choosing solitude, he acquired great public influence; teaching humility, he found himself obliged to correct both popes and kings. While hot to enter a dispute wherever he believed that wrong had been committed, his pent-up energies, like a peal of thunder, quickly cleared the air, and he was at once able to return to the sober calm of common sense: his quick resentment harboured no lingering fires. The real man, in all his simplicity and tenderness, was jealousy shielded by an aversion to any display of sentiment; but in rare unguarded moments, he was found playing with a little girl at her father's villa, or sending to one of his monks the kiss, which in the haste of exile he had omitted to bestow. The poor, the sick and unfortunate were drawn to him by his sharing in their common lot; even criminals, released from their fetters, felt impelled to kneel beside him as he prayed; and rough soldiers asked his pardon when they came to him from Luxeuil. A gentle warmth of understanding, combined with a fervent faith, caused him to be credited with strange powers of healing, both for the body and the soul; remarkable predictions, guided in part by the shrewdness of his political observation, clothed him with the mysterious interest of a seer. Except for the more pedantic type of punning, he was devoid of humour; yet the very tenderness of his natural melancholy rendered him attractive to all classes of society, so the noblemen entrusted him with their sons' education, and kings and courtiers were ready to welcome his reproof. At home with all men, he rested nowhere; capable of all tasks, he set his heart on self-denial. Scholarship had failed to impress its objective balance on the poetic ardour of his nature, and solitude led him to seek truth on the side of the minority; once he entered on a quarrel, his courage never flinched at odds.

Great strength of body matched his strength of mind, his openness of manner did not belie the beauty of his face; but an abstract devotion to principle tended to blight his warm spirit with the chill of a precision. Lacking originality, his talents were best suited to the quiet of the cloister, yet sheer determination made him an outstanding leader of his age. A character so complex and so contrary, humble and haughty, harsh and tender, pedantic and impetuous by turns, had as its guiding and unifying pattern the ambition of sainthood. All his activities were subordinate to this one end, and with the self-sacrifice that can seem so close to self-assertion, he worked out his soul's salvation by the one sure pathway that he knew. He was a missionary through circumstance, a monk by vocation; a contemplative, too frequently driven to action by the world; a pilgrim, on the road to Paradise.

PART 2

Writings

Introduction

All Columban's surviving writings are in Latin. As several of them refer to the controversies in which he took part or mention some of his contemporaries by name, they enable us to add certain biographical details to the basic material derived from Jonas. Through them, also, several aspects of the man's outlook and personality shine forth more clearly – his innate conservatism and suspicion of innovations, his respect for the papacy, his contempt for riches and power, his outspokenness, his loving care for his friends.

It is tragic, though, that so many of his writings have perished. The most serious loss is surely his commentary on the Psalter which Jonas says he composed at an early age. Copies survived for centuries after his death, and the St Gallen library possessed one in the ninth century, as did Bobbio in the tenth. Columban himself mentions in his letters the three 'volumes' he addressed to Pope Gregory, the summary he sent to Arigius and the treatise he wrote on *The Three Chapters* – all these have likewise disappeared. We have now only one of his several letters to Pope Gregory. Jonas mentions a treatise written in Milan against the Arians and letters to Frankish kings, Theuderich and Clothair, but no trace of any of these is known to survive. Yet the volume of his surviving writings is still impressive and places him head and shoulders above all his contemporaries as the first great Irish man of letters.

This title should perhaps have gone to his earlier namesake of Iona were all *his* writings preserved, but so few of the verses attributed to the latter can go back to his pen in their surviving form that he is left with only a couple of Latin poems with which to challenge the Bobbio saint.

Columban's writings fall naturally into four categories: 1. Monastic Rules and Penitential, 2. Letters, 3. Sermons, 4. Poetry. These works have appeared in several editions, and one remarkable Irish name, which must definitely be mentioned in connection with them, is that of the seventeenth-century Franciscan from Co. Louth, Fr Patrick Fleming, who with Louvain as his starting-point travelled over much of Europe and searched in monasteries and libraries for material of Columbanian interest. He visited Bobbio in 1623 and by 1630 his great work on Columban was in the printer's hands. Then his own untimely death intervened, and it was only in 1667 that Fleming's *Collectanea Sacra* was published by Fr Thomas Sheerin.

Of the more recent editions of the writings of Columban, that by the Abbé Migne in his *Patrologia Latina* vol. 80 gave the Irish saint a place among the Western Fathers in all the great libraries of the world, but made no attempt to establish a critical text or to separate his genuine writings from others which later generations attributed to him. These were the tasks which a group of German scholars set themselves at the end of the last century: Dümmler who edited the Rowing Song as early as 1881 (but attributed it to an otherwise unknown Columbanus of the Carolingian period), Gundlach who published the remainder of the poems as well as the prose letters in the *Monumenta Germaniae Historica, Epistolae* in 1892, and Seebass who edited a few of the sermons, the two monastic Rules and the Penitential in a German Church history periodical between 1894 and 1897. With these may be linked their fellow-countryman Bruno Krusch, who published in *MGH* in 1902 (reissued in an improved form in 1905) what still remains the standard critical edition of Columban's life by Jonas. A new edition of Jonas, based on one MS only (ed. M. Tosi), was published in Italy in 1965.

All these editions of Columban's writing have been superseded in our own day by the splendid volume *Sancti Columbani Opera*, edited by Dr G.S.M. Walker and published by the Dublin Institute for Advanced Studies in 1957. Not only does it make all Columban's writings available in a single handy volume for the first time, but in thoroughness of research and felicity of presentation it attains a standard which will not easily be surpassed. The Latin texts reproduced here are taken from Walker's admirable volume, and my translations are deeply indebted to his pioneer versions. As my book is meant for the general reader, however, I felt at liberty to give a much freer rendering of the Latin than is to be found in Walker's book.

Two further modern editions of Columban's Penitential must also, of course, be mentioned: Dom Jean Laporte's *Le Pénitential de Saint Columban* (Tournai, 1958) and Dr Ludwig Bieler's *The Irish Penitentials* (Dublin Institute for Advanced Studies, 1963), both works of the highest critical standards.

It would be ungracious to conclude this short introduction to the writings of St Columban without calling attention to the highly stimulating work *Studies on the language and style of Columba the Younger* (Columbanus), by J.W. Smit (Amsterdam, 1971). Smit challenges the attribution of the Columbanus poems to Columban of Bobbio, and this part of his book will be dealt with later in treating of Columban's poetry. Here it will be sufficient to add that Smit also provides a critical interpretation and translation of several of the more difficult passages in the prose letters and suggests some emendations. This part of his work has been very helpful to me and I have followed his interpretations in a number of the passages translated below.

I.

Monastic Rules and Penitential

Two Rules are attributed to St Columban: the *Regula Monachorum* or Rule of the Monks and the *Regula Coenobialis* or Community Rule. Each Rule is found in a number of manuscripts which go back to the ninth or tenth century. The *Regula Coenobialis* was later expanded to include material from Columban's successors in Luxeuil; the *Regula Monachorum* was subsequently shortened by the omission of material which was no longer relevant. It follows therefore that the whole of the latter, but only a portion of the former, comes from the pen of Columban.

The Penitential of St Columban is one of the most valuable documents in existence for a study of the doctrine of penance in the Irish Church. It made a system of private penance available to the laity as well as to the monks, and, as it was the earliest penitential in the Irish tradition to be employed on the continent, it had a significant influence on the development there of the new theology of the Sacrament of Penance.

All three documents are written in a somewhat arid Latinity, in sharp contrast to the rhetorical and imaginative style of Columban's other writings.

The Rule of the Monks
St Columban's Rule for his monks is a broad treatise on the basic virtues of obedience, poverty, chastity, mortification,

silence, etc. in the monastery, rather than a list of detailed regulations concerning daily life. Laporte has suggested that the early chapters are a summary of a work composed in Bangor by Comgall. The Rule is strict in its demands but its tone is balanced and tolerant throughout. With the exception of one long chapter laying down regulations for the recitation of the Divine Office and some prescriptions regarding food and drink, the Rule is exclusively concerned with the interior dispositions of the soul. In this, Columban's Rule differed enormously from the detailed regulations laid down in the Rule of St Benedict.

A sample of the *Regula Monachorum* is the chapter which deals with the meals of the monks:

The food of the monks should be poor and confined to the evening; let it be such as to avoid gorging, and their drink such as to avoid drunkenness, so that it may sustain them but do them no harm: vegetables, beans, flour mixed with water, along with a small loaf of bread, lest the stomach be strained and the mind stifled. For those who seek eternal rewards should only take account of a thing's usefulness and use. Use of life must be kept under control, just as work must be kept under control. This is true discretion, so that the possibility of spiritual progress may be maintained with an abstinence that scourges the flesh. For if abstinence goes too far, it will be a vice, not a virtue. A virtue tolerates and embraces many material things. Therefore we must fast daily, just as we must feed daily. While we must eat daily, we must regale the body rather poorly and sparingly. The reason we must eat daily is because we must advance daily, pray daily, toil daily, and read daily.

The Community Rule

Like the Rule of the Monks, the *Regula Coenobialis* was drawn up for one of Columban's monastic communities, possibly a different one from that which received the previous Rule. Walker takes chapters I to IX of this Rule to contain the nucleus which goes back to Columban himself; he would regard the later chapters of the shorter recension and the extra interpolations of the longer recension as having been added by Columban's successors in Luxeuil. These show some relaxation of the stricter prescriptions found in the earlier part.

This Rule provides a more detailed commentary on the daily life of an early Irish monk than any other source. Yet even here a lack of systematisation is obvious, and the *Regula Coenobialis* would seem to have grown out of a collection of practical decisions given in the case of the breaches of discipline rather than being a conscious effort to draw up systematic regulations to order the whole life of the monastery.

As a sample of the *Regula Coenobialis*, chapters III–V, which deal with the omission of prayers, disrespect for sacred things and abuses of speech, are included here:

> The monk who does not prostrate himself to ask a prayer when leaving the house, and after receiving a blessing does not bless himself, and go to the cross – it is prescribed to correct him with twelve blows.
>
> Likewise the one who shall forget the prayer before work or after work – with twelve blows.
>
> He who on his return home does not prostrate himself within the house to ask a prayer, is to be corrected with twelve blows. But the brother who confesses all these things and more, even as much as to deserve a grace penance, gets off with half penance, that is, a medium penance; and so on with these matters. Mitigate them thus for the moment.

The monk who through coughing goes wrong in the chant at the beginning of a psalm – it is laid down to correct him with six blows. Likewise the one who bites the cup of salvation with his teeth – with six blows.

The one who does not follow the order for the sacrifice – with six blows.

The one who smiles at the synaxis, that is, at the office of prayers – with six blows; if he bursts out laughing aloud – with a grave penance unless it happens excusably.

The one who receives the blessed bread with unclean hands – with twelve blows.

He who forgets to make the oblation until he goes to Mass – with a hundred blows.

The monk who tells idle tales to another, if he censures himself at once – with a mere pardon, but if he does not censure himself – with an imposition in silence or fifty blows.

He who defends himself truthfully, when questioned about something, and does not at once beg pardon and say 'It's my fault, I'm sorry' – with fifty blows.

He who in all honesty sets counsel against counsel – with fifty blows.

He who strikes the altar – with fifty blows.

He who shouts loud talk without restraint, unless there is need – with an imposition of silence or fifty blows. He who makes an excuse in order to get pardon must do a like penance.

He who replies to a brother on his pointing something out 'It's not as you say,' except for seniors speaking frankly to juniors – with an imposition of silence or fifty blows.

The only exception to this permitted is that he may answer a brother of equal standing if he remembers something nearer the truth than what the latter says.

The Penitential

The Irish Penitentials contain lists of the various ways in which people are liable to commit sin, together with the penance considered appropriate for each. The earliest Irish one which has survived is the Penitential of Vinnian, who is to be identified with either Finnian of Clonard (d.549) or Finnian of Moville (d.579).

The Penitential of Columban shows considerable dependence on that of Vinnian. Contrary to the opinion of some other scholars, Dom Jean Laporte has demonstrated that it is a single document which however falls into three parts, one for monks, one for the secular clergy and one for the laity. Apart from a few paragraphs added later, there is no reason to question Columban's authorship of the document as a whole. It probably dates from his early period on the Continent in Annegray or Luxeuil.

The penances imposed by the Irish Penitentials as a whole seem severe to our modern outlook and Columban's Penitential is no exception. The following excerpts, taken from the section dealing with the laity, will indicate the length and severity of penances to be imposed for sins of theft, perjury, wounding and drunkenness. Yet compared with the more vindictive penalties of public and perpetual excommunications enforced in earlier centuries, they offered to the penitent the hope of reconciliation and re-admission to the sacraments after the period of penance was over:

If any layman commits theft, that is, steals an ox or a horse or a sheep or any beast of his neighbour's, if he has done it once or twice, he must first restore to his neighbour the loss which he has caused, and let him do penance for a hundred and twenty days on bread and water. But if he has made a practice of stealing often, and is unable to make a restitution, let him do penance for a year and a hundred and twenty days, and let him further promise not to do it again. He may go to Communion at Easter of the second year, that is, after two years, on condition that, out of his own labour, he first gives alms to the poor and a feast to the priest who adjudged his penance. Thus is the guilt of his bad habit to be removed.

If any layman commits perjury, if he does it through greed, he is to sell all his goods and give to the poor, and dedicate himself wholly to the Lord. Let him abandon the world and be tonsured and let him serve God till death in a monastery. But if he does it, not through greed, but for fear of death, he must do penance for three years on bread and water in exile and unarmed. For two more let him abstain from wine and meats; then let him offer a life for himself, that is, let him free a slave or maidservant from the yoke of bondage, and give alms frequently for two years. During this period he may quite lawfully use all foods except meat. Let him go to Communion after the seventh year.

If any of the laity sheds blood in a squabble, or wounds or maims his neighbour, he is to be forced to make good the damage he has done. If he has not the wherewith to pay, let him first carry in his neighbour's work, as long as the latter is sick, and send for the doctor. After the man's recovery, let him do penance for forty days on bread and water.

If any layman becomes drunk, or eats or drinks to the point of vomiting, let him do penance for a week on bread and water.

II.
LETTERS

S ix letters of Columban have survived; a number of others, of whose former existence we are certain, have now perished. A seventh letter, sometimes attributed to him because it concerns the Easter controversy, can scarcely be his and has been relegated by Walker to an appendix. The sixth letter below is in a different style from the others and its MS tradition also differs from theirs. It contains no formal address and is more in the nature of an exhortation, which is the title given to it in some of the sources.

The six letters may be listed as follows in the order in which they were written:

1. To Pope Gregory the Great, written probably in 600.
2. To the French Bishops meeting in Chalon, 603.
3. To a newly elected Pope, either Pope Sabinian in 604 or, less probably, Pope Boniface III in 607.
4. To his monks in Luxeuil and neighbourhood, written in Nantes in 610 as he awaited expulsion from France.
5. To Pope Boniface IV, written in Milan in 613.
6. To a young disciple – addressee and date unknown. (It may have been written in 610 to either Domoal or Chagnoald, both of whom acted as his minister). The Easter controversy figures largely in Letters 1, 2 and 3 and is mentioned in passing in Letter 4. Columban's epistolary

style is marked by a complex word-order, frequent use of alliteration, proverbs and puns, and the appearance of some rare words derived from Greek. The letters are all long, with one exception, and even at times long-winded; they have a preaching tone about them which makes them akin to his sermons. In their Latinity however they are carefully composed by an author who could be trenchant and persuasive in turn without departing from the niceties of style which good rhetoric demanded. Only some excerpts from each letter are given here.

Letter to Pope Gregory the Great, 600 AD

Grace and peace to you from God our Father and from our Lord Jesus Christ.

I wish, Holy Father (do not think it excessive of me), to ask about Easter, in accordance with that verse of Scripture: 'Ask your father and he will show you, your elders and they will tell you.' When an unworthy man like me writes to an illustrious one like yourself, my insignificance makes applicable to me the striking remark which a certain philosopher is said to have once made on seeing a painted harlot: 'I do not admire the art, but I admire the cheek.' Nevertheless I take the liberty of writing to you, strengthened by the assurance of your evangelical humility and I append the cause of my grief. For one has no reason to boast of writing when necessity demands it, even if the writing is to one's superiors.

I have read your book containing the pastoral rule, brief in style, comprehensive in doctrine, crammed with sacred things. I acknowledge that the work is sweeter than honey to one in need. In my thirst therefore I beg you for Christ's sake to present me with your tracts on Ezekiel, which I heard you composed with remarkable skill. I have read six books of Jerome on him;

but he did not expound even half. But, if you please, send me something from your lectures delivered in the city. I mean the last things expounded in the book. Send as well the Song of Songs from that passage in which it says: 'I will go to the mountain of myrrh and to the hill of incense' as far as the end. Treat it, I pray, either with others' comments or with your own in brief. In order to expound all the obscurity of Zechariah, reveal his secrets, so that in these matters the blindness of the West may give you thanks. Everyone knows my demands are pressing, my inquiries wide. But your resources are also great, for you know well that from a small stock less should be lent, and 'from a large one more'.

Let charity move you to reply. Don't let the sharpness of this letter keep you from explaining things, since anger explodes into error, and it is my heart's desire to pay you due honour. My part was the challenge, to question, to beg; let yours be not to deny what you have freely received, to bend your talent to the seeker, and to give the bread of doctrine according to Christ's command. Peace to you and yours. Please pardon my rashness, Holy Father, for having written so boldly. I beseech you to pray for me, a most wretched sinner, even once in your holy prayers to our common Lord.

Letter to the French Bishops, 603 AD
Great harm has been done and is being done to the peace of the Church by different usages and diverse traditions. But if, as I have said, we first hasten by the exercise of true humility to cure the poisons of pride and envy and vainglory, through the teaching of our Saviour who says for our example: 'Learn of me for I am meek and humble of heart,' etc., then when we have been made perfect, with no further blemish and with hatred rooted out, let us all, as the disciples of our Lord Jesus Christ, love one

another with our whole hearts. If there are diverse traditions as is the case regarding Easter ... let us see which is the more true tradition – yours, or that of your (Irish) brothers in the West. For, as I have noted in the book giving my answer, which I have now sent you, though it was written three years ago, all the churches of the entire West consider that the resurrection should not take place before the passion, that is, Easter before the Equinox. They do not wait beyond the twentieth of the moon, lest they should perform a sacrament of the New Testament without the authority of the Old. But this I leave to another time. Besides, I have informed the Holy Father in three books of their opinions about Easter, and in a short pamphlet I have further taken the liberty of writing the same to your holy brother Arigius.

One thing therefore I request of you, holy men: with peace and charity bear with my ignorance and, as some call it, my arrogant insolence in writing. Necessity, not pride, is the cause of it, as my own worthlessness proves. I am not the author of this variance and it is for Christ the Saviour, our common Lord and God, that I have come to these lands as a pilgrim. I beseech you therefore by our common Lord, and beg of you by him who will judge the living and the dead, if you deserve to be recognised by him who will say to many: 'Amen, I say to you that I never knew you,' to allow me with your peace and charity to remain in silence in these woods and to live beside the bones of our seventeen dead brethren, just as up till now we have been allowed to live twelve years among you. This will allow us, as we have done up to the present, to pray for you as we ought. Let Gaul, I pray, contain us together, whom the kingdom of heaven shall contain, if our merits are good. We have one kingdom promised and one hope for our calling in Christ. We shall reign together with him, if we first suffer with him here so that with him we may be glorified.

I know that to many this long-windedness of mine will seem overdone. But I decided it was better to let you know what we are discussing and thinking here among ourselves. For our rules are the commandments of the Lord and the apostles. In them our confidence is placed. They are our weapons, shield and sword. These are our defence. They brought us from our native land. We strive after them here, too, though lukewarmly. We pray and hope to continue until death in them as we have seen our predecessors do. But, holy fathers, see what you are doing to poor veterans and aged pilgrims. In my opinion it will be better for you to support them than disturb them.

For the rest, fathers, pray for us as we also do for you, wretched though we be, and don't look on us as aliens from you. For we are all fellow members of one body, whether Franks or Britons or Irish or whatever our race. Thus let all our races rejoice in knowledge of the faith and in recognising the Son of God. Let us all hasten to approach to perfect manhood, to the measure of the age of fullness of Jesus Christ. In him let us love one another, praise one another, correct one another, encourage one another, pray for one another, so that with him and one another we may reign and triumph. Pardon me, I pray, for being long-winded and presumptuous. I am labouring beyond my strength, most patient and holy fathers and brethren.

Letter to the newly elected Pope, 604 or 607 AD

Give us your opinion; it will be a sweet consolation to us pilgrims in our labours. You will thus confirm, if it is not contrary to the faith, the tradition of our predecessors. Thereby we shall be able through your decision to observe in our pilgrimage the rite of Easter as we have received it from our ancestors. For it is clear that we are in our native land as long as we accept no rules of those Franks. We stay in seclusion, harming no one. We abide by the rules of our predecessors. It was to defend these that we wrote both of you, apostolic father, as I have said, and to your brethren, our neighbours and our fathers in Christ, those letters which this note commends to you. We cannot do justice to the merits of the case, as our opponents indulge more in rage than reason. But we now at the opportune moment ask for the vote which your authority can give so that with a decision we may be able to live amongst those men with the peace of Church unity. This is what the holy fathers, namely Polycarp and Pope Anicetus, taught – to live without offence to the faith, nay preserving in perfect charity – each retaining what he has received and 'remaining wherein he has been called'.

Farewell, Pope most dear in Christ. Remember us, both in your holy prayers beside the ashes of the saints, and in your most dutiful decisions, following the hundred and fifty authorities of the Council of Constantinople, who decided that churches of God planted in pagan nations should live by their own laws, as they had been taught by their fathers.

Letter to the monks of Luxeuil, 610 AD

My dearest Attala, you know those who from your point of view are a nuisance. Remove them at once, you get rid of them in peace and agreement with the Rule. But promote Libranus and always hold on to Waldelenus. If he is there with the community, may God be good to him. May he be humble; and give him my kiss which in the hurry he did not receive.

You know for long how my purpose was to build up character. If you see that souls make progress there, stay there. If you see dangers, come away. The dangers I mean are the dangers of discord. I'm afraid of disagreement there on account of Easter, lest perhaps, through the devil's tricks, they may wish to banish you, if you do not keep peace with them. Without me you now seem to stand more weakly there. Therefore be wary, considering 'the time they do not endure sound doctrine'. Instruct yourselves and all who may be willing to listen; only let there be none amongst you who is not united. For you (Attala) must chiefly strive for peace, 'ever anxious to preserve unity of spirit in the bond of peace'. What good is it to have a body and not to have a heart?

I'm broken, I confess, for this reason: while I wished to help all, 'when I spoke to them they fought against me without cause', and while I trusted all, I was almost made a fool. Let you be wiser. I don't wish you to undertake so great a task, under which I sweated; for you know already how tiny was my knowledge, just a drop. You have learnt that all warnings are not suitable for all, since natures are diverse and the characters of people differ widely among themselves. But what am I doing? I'll soon be urging you to that huge task from which I'm flying myself. If I go on to diversity of doctrine, I'll stay within bounds. Therefore let you be many-sided and adaptable to the direction of those who obey you with faith and love. But you must fear even their very love, because it will be dangerous to you.

Now that I write a messenger has arrived with the news that the ship is ready for me. By it I'll be carried unwillingly to my homeland. If I flee, however, there's no guard to prevent it, for they seem to want me to escape. If I'm cast into the sea like Jonah, which is the Hebrew name for Columba, pray that someone in place of the whale may hide me safely and bring me back on a happy voyage, to restore your Jonah to the land he longs for.

But now I must end this parchment letter, though the vastness of my subject requires a more extensive treatment. Love doesn't keep order, hence my missive is confused. I wanted to say everything briefly, but couldn't manage everything. I was unwilling to write what I wanted to write in view of your diverse wishes. Perhaps my own will is not without its attraction; God's will be done in all things. If he will, he knows my desire. Examine your consciences, whether you are more pure and holy in my absence. Don't seek me through love, but through necessity alone. May you be no poorer by this event, and don't through this parting seek a freedom that would make you slave to the vices. He who loves unity is mine; he who divides is not mine, for 'he who does not gather with me,' says the Lord, 'scatters.'

Moreover, if you see perfection further removed from you than before, and fate keeps me away from you, and Attala is not strong enough to govern you, then as your brethren are here in the neighbourhood of the Britons, unite yourselves all together in one group, whichever is the better, that you may more easily fight against the vices and snares of the devil. Meanwhile let the man whom you all have elected be over you: because if I'm free to do so, I'll take care of you, God willing. But if the locality pleases you and God builds with you there, 'increase to thousands of thousands' there with his blessing. Pray for me, my own children, that I may live to God.

Letter to Pope Boniface IV, 613 AD

I grieve, I confess, for the disgrace of St Peter's chair. Yet I know that the affair is beyond me, and that at the first frown I am, as the saying goes, putting my face under the coals. But what do I care about saving face before men, when zeal for the faith needs to be shown? Before God and angels I shall be undaunted; it is praiseworthy to be embarrassed before men for God's sake. If I'm listened to, the gain will be shared; if I'm ignored, mine will be the rap.

I'll speak as a friend, a disciple, and one who follows in your footsteps, not as a stranger. Therefore I'll speak out freely, and say to those who are our captains and pilots and mystical watches of the spiritual ship: 'Look out, for the sea is stormy and is being lashed by fatal gusts.' For a ninth particularly threatening wave has also been churned into a raging sea and still swelling up from afar, is borne from the foaming whirlpools of a hollow rock (perhaps I exaggerate) and is driving before it the ship which has ploughed through eight storms already. It is a tempest of the entire element, surging up everywhere and convulsed on every side, that threatens the mystical vessel with shipwreck. Hence I, a frightened sailor, dare to scream: 'Look out, for water has already entered the vessel of the Church, and the ship is in peril.'

For all we Irish, inhabitants of the world's edge, are disciples of Saint Peter and Paul and of all the disciples who wrote the sacred canon by the Holy Spirit. We accept nothing outside the evangelical and apostolic teaching. None of us was a heretic, no one a Jew, no one a schismatic; but the Catholic faith, as it was first transmitted by you (the Popes), successors of the holy apostles, is maintained unbroken.

Strengthened and urged on by this assurance I have dared to stir you up against those who insult you and call you the supporters of heretics and name you schismatics, so that my boasting, with which I answered them confidently on your behalf, may not be in vain, and so that they, not us, may be confounded. I declared on your behalf that the Roman Church defends no heretic against the Catholic faith – that is how disciples should feel for their master. Therefore accept with willing mind and dutiful ears this necessary presumptuous interference of mine. Anything useful or orthodox that I say will redound to you; for his disciples' teaching is a credit to the master. If a son speaks wisely, his father will rejoice, and yours will be the credit, because as I said, it has come from you. Purity redounds, not to the river, but to its source. But if you find any confused words of excessive zeal, either in his letter or in the other against Agrippinus, who provoked me into writing, attribute it to my lack of discretion, not to arrogance.

If any of my words have outwardly caused offence to pious ears, pardon me for my treatment of such rugged passages, as a historical account of the events permits me to omit nothing from my inquiry, and the freedom of my country's customs, so to speak, was in part the cause of my boldness. For among us it is not who you are but how you make your case that counts. Love for the peace of the Gospel forces me to tell all in order to shame both of you who ought to have been one choir. Another reason is my great concern for your harmony and peace. 'For if one member suffers, all the members suffer with it.'

As I have said before, we are bound to the Chair of St Peter. Though Rome be great and famous, she is great and renowned among us only because of that Chair. The name of the city which is Italy's glory is something most sacred and widely divorced from prosaic spots on earth, a city once founded to the great joy of nearly every nation. The name has been spread far and wide through the whole world, as far as the Western regions on the edge of the earth, and, wonderful to relate, the ocean's surging floods leaping and whirling mightily on all sides did not prevent this. Yet from the time that the Son of God deigned to be man it rode over the sea of nations on those two most fiery steeds of God's spirit (I mean the apostles Peter and Paul, whose dear relics have made you blessed); it troubled many waters and enlarged his chariots with countless thousands of people. Thus the Most High Driver of that chariot (who is Christ, the true Father, the Charioteer of Israel) came over the channels' surge, over the dolphins' backs, over the swelling flood, and reached even unto us.

From that time you are great and famous, and Rome herself is nobler and more famed. If it may be said that you are almost heavenly beings because of Christ's twin apostles (I speak of those whom the Holy Spirit called 'heavens declaring the glory of God', to whom is applied that text: 'Their voice has gone out into every land and their words to the ends of the earth'), then Rome is also head of the Churches of the world, saving the special prerogative of the place of the Lord's Resurrection. Thus, as your honour is great in proportion to the dignity of your See, you need to take equally great care not to lose your reputation through some error. Power will rest with you just so long as your principles remain sound. The real key-bearer of the kingdom of Heaven is he who opens up true knowledge to the worthy and shuts to the unworthy. If on the other hand he does the opposite, he will be able neither to open nor to shut.

Therefore, my dearest friends, come to an agreement quickly and meet together and don't argue over ancient quarrels. Rather keep quiet and consign them to eternal silence and oblivion. If any things are doubtful, leave them to God's judgement. The things which are clear, which men can decide, give your verdict on these justly and without favouritism. 'Let there be peaceful judgement in your gates', and pardon one another, that there may be 'joy in heaven' and on earth because of your peace and concord. Why should you defend anything but the Catholic faith if you are true Christians on both sides? I can't understand how a Christian can quarrel with a Christian about the faith. Whatever an orthodox Christian who rightly glorifies the Lord will say, the other will answer Amen, because he also loves and believes alike. 'Let you therefore all say and think the one thing' so that both sides 'may be one' – all Christians.

As a sample of Columban's prose style I append the original Latin of the first section of those passages from the letter to Pope Boniface which have been translated here. It shows the elaborate form of rhetoric which he cultivated, with many of the devices – rhetorical questions, intercalated verbs, idiomatic expressions, biblical echoes, prolongation of metaphors, parallel phrases contrasted with each other – which were the stock-in-trade of the great preachers of Christian antiquity.

Doleo enim, fateor, de infamia cathedrae sancti Petri; scio tamen super me esse negotium, et quod prima fronte sub prunas, ut dicitur, faciem ponam. Sed quid mihi facies coram hominibus, ubi zelus fidei prodi necesse est? Coram Deo et angelis non confundar; laus est pro Deo coram hominibus confundi. Si exaudiar, commune lucrum erit; si despiciar, mea merces erit. Ego enim ut amicus, ut discipulus, ut pedisequus vester, non ut alienus loquar; ideo libere eloquar nostris utpote magistris ac spiritalis navis gubernatoribus ac mysticis proretis, dicens, Vigilate, quia mare procellosum est et flabris exasperatur feralibus, quia nona sola minax unda, quae etiam permota in pontum semper cautis spumosis concavae vorticibus (hyperbolice licet) de longe turgescens extollitur et ante se carbasa sulcatis octo molibus trudit, sed tempestas totius elementi nimirum undique consurgentis et undique commoti mysticae navis naufragium intentat; ideo audeo timidus nauta clamare, Vigilante, quia aqua iam intravit in ecclesiae navem et navis periclitatur. Nos enimsanctorum Petri et Pauli et omnium discipulorum divinum canonem spiritu sancto scribentium discipuli sumus, toti Iberi, ultimi habitatores mundi, nihil extra evangelicam et apostolicam doctrinam recipientes; nullus hereticus, nullus Iudaeus, nullus schismaticus fuit; sed fides catholica, sicut a vobis primum, sanctorum videlicet apostolorum successoribus, tradita est, inconcussa tenetur. (*Here I have accepted Smit's text where it differs from Walker's.*)

Letter to a young disciple, c. 610 AD

Be helpful when you are at the bottom of the ladder and be the lowest when you are in authority. Be simple in faith but well trained in manners; demanding in your own affairs but unconcerned in those of others. Be guileless in friendship, astute in the face of deceit, tough in times of ease, tender in hard times. Keep your options open when there's no problem, but dig in when you must choose. Be pleasant when things are unpleasant, and sorrowful when they are pleasant. Disagree where necessary, but be in agreement about truth. Be serious in pleasures but kindly when things are bitter. Be strong in trials, weak in dissensions. Be slow to anger, quick to learn, also slow to speak, as St James says, equally quick to listen. Be up and doing to make progress, slack to take revenge, careful in word, eager in work. Be friendly with men of honour, stiff with rascals, gentle to the weak, firm to the stubborn, steadfast to the proud, humble to the lowly. Be ever sober, ever chaste, ever modest. Be patient as far as compatible with zeal, never greedy, always generous, if not in money, then in spirit. Be timely in fasting, timely in the night-offices, discreet in duty, persistent in study, unshaken in turmoil, joyful in suffering, valiant in the cause of truth, cautious in time of strife. Be submissive to good, unbending to evil, gentle in generosity, untiring in love, just in all things. Be respectful to the worthy, respectful to the poor. Be mindful of favours, unmindful of wrongs. Be a lover of the ordinary man, and don't wish for riches, but cool down excitement and speak your mind. Obey your seniors, keep up with your juniors, equal your equals, emulate the perfect. Don't envy your betters, or grieve at those who surpass you, or censure those who fall behind, but agree with those who urge you on. Though weary, don't give up. Weep and rejoice at the one time out of zeal and hope. Advance with determination, but always fear for the end.

III.

SERMONS

Thirteen sermons are accepted by Walker as genuine works of the Irish saint; two others, for which the manuscript evidence is not so convincing, are regarded by him as doubtful. Laporte claims to have found fragments of further sermons composed by St Columban, but no complete work. On the other hand it must be added that the authenticity of the great majority of the thirteen sermons was challenged in the past by two distinguished German scholars, Hauck and Seebass. Their arguments have been countered by Walker, who finds several echoes in these sermons of Columban's writings and calls attention to the similarity between the biblical text quoted in the sermons and elsewhere in the saint's works. More recently Smit, without going into the question in detail, regards Columban's authorship of all these sermons as doubtful.

Walker supposes that the whole series of thirteen sermons forms a unit and that they were preached in Milan by St Columban in 613. This would explain the concentration of Sermon 1 on the doctrine of the Trinity which was one of the central points at issue in the Arian controversies. The Sermons are couched in a rhetorical style similar to that of the Letters but with more restraint and less striving for effect. As the same train of thought runs through many of the sermons, a few excerpts will suffice to introduce the reader to this part of Columban's work. I have translated one sermon in full (Sermon

V) and passages from two others. Between them they illustrate three of his preaching moods – the doctrinal instruction, the moral exhortation and the mystical prayer.

Sermon 1: On faith

Who then is God? He is Father, Son and Holy Spirit, yet one God. Seek no further concerning God; for those who wish to know the great deep must first study the nature of things. Knowledge of the Trinity is properly compared to the depth of the sea, according to that saying of the Sage: 'And the great deep, who shall discover it?' If then a man wishes to know the deepest ocean of divine understanding, let him first, if he is able, scan that visible sea. The less he finds his knowledge to be of those sea creatures which lurk beneath the sea, the more he should realise his ignorance of the depths of its Creator. As he must and should do, let him dare to treat less of the Creator than of the creature, since none can be qualified in the greater who has not first examined the less. And when a man is not trusted in the lesser, how is he to be trusted in the greater? Why, I ask, does a man who doesn't know earthly things examine the heavenly?

Oh, those who speak idle words, according to the Apostle, 'they know neither what they speak, nor what things they affirm!' How many indeed (to whom it is woe) though straining to fly aloft with feeble wing, and setting their creature's face towards the sky (at least in part, not to say in every case) without having assembled the arguments beforehand, dare with unclean heart and impure lips to teach first concerning the great deep! They don't understand that it is not by words but by faith that God the Trinity is known. He is understood by the pious faith of a pure heart, and not by the rantings of a wicked mouth. Therefore the great Trinity is to be piously believed and not wickedly discussed, for the One Triune God is an ocean that cannot be crossed or explored. High is the heaven, broad the earth, deep the sea and long the ages; but higher and broader and deeper and longer is his knowledge. For he has been adorned by nature, he who created it from nothing.

Sermon V: On human life

Oh human life, fragile and mortal. How many have you deceived! How many have you inveigled! How many have you blinded! Though you fly, you are nothing. Though you are seen, you are but a shadow. Daily you depart and daily you commence. When you are coming, you are going, and when you are going, you are coming, unequal at the end, alike at the beginning, unequal in pleasure, alike in passing away; sweet to the stupid, bitter to the wise. Those who love you don't know you, and those who despise you really understand you. Therefore you are not true but false. You display yourself as true; you prove yourself false.

What then are you, human life? You are the road of mortals and not their life, with sin at the beginning and death at the end. You would have been a true life if the sin of man's first transgression hadn't shattered you. Then you became fragile and mortal, and marked all your travellers for death. So you are the road to life, not life itself; you are a real road but not a level one, long for some, short for others, broad for some, narrow for others, joyful for some, sad for others, for all alike fleeting and irrevocable. A road is what you are, a road; but you are not clear to all. Many see you, and few understand you to be a road. For you are so wily and so enticing that few know you as a road. Therefore you are to be questioned but not believed and given bail; you are to be traversed but not inhabited, wretched human life. For no one dwells on a road, but travels it, so that those who walk upon the road may dwell in their homeland.

Why then, mortal life, are you dwelt in, loved and protected by the stupid and the lost, but despised by men of sense and guarded against by those that shall be saved? You have to be feared and shunned a great deal, human life, you are so fleeting, so slippery, so dangerous, so short, so uncertain, that you'll vanish like a shadow or a mirage or a cloud, of nothingness or emptiness. Thus while you are nothing, mortal life, except a road, a mirage, fleeting and void, or a cloud, vague and feeble, and a shadow like a dream, we must journey along you so anxiously, so carefully, so speedily, that all intelligent men should hurry like travellers to their true homeland, sure of the past, but worried by what still remains.

It is no gain to you to climb the heights you have climbed, unless you get safely past what remains; for this life is to be considered as a road and an ascent. Let us not seek en route what shall be in our homeland. Therefore we must beware lest perhaps we be carefree on the way, and fail to reach our true homeland.

Some are really so careless on this journey, that they seem to be not so much en route as at home. They travel reluctantly rather than willingly towards a homeland that is surely already lost. They have used up their home here on the road and for a brief life have bought eternal death. Unhappy men, they enjoy their disappointed trading; they have loved the perishable goods of others, and neglected their own eternal good. Hence, however enjoyable these be, however alluring, however dazzling, let us avoid the earthly good of others, that we may not lose our own eternal good. Let us be found faithful in regard to the goods of others, so that in respect of our own private goods we may be made heirs by the gift of our Lord Jesus Christ, who lives and reigns forever and ever. Amen.

Sermon XII: On remorse

Lord, grant me, I pray you, in the name of Jesus Christ, your Son, my God, the charity that does not fail, so that my lamp may be always lighted, never extinguished, and may burn for me and give light to others. Christ, kindle our lamps, our Saviour most sweet to us, that they may always shine in your temple and continually receive light from you, the Light Perpetual, so that our own darkness may be illuminated and the darkness of the world expelled from us. Give my lamp such a share of your light, my Jesus, I pray, that its brightness may reveal to me the Holy of Holies, where you the eternal Priest of all eternity enter the portals of your great temple, so that I may always gaze at, behold and desire only you. May I love and contemplate you alone and may my lamp ever burn and shine before you.

I beseech you, most loving Saviour, show yourself to us who seek you, so that knowing you we may love you as warmly in return – may love you alone, desire you alone, contemplate you alone by day and night and keep you always in our thoughts. Inspire us with a love for you as great as the affection and attachment which is due to you as our God. May affection for you pervade our hearts. May attachment to you take possession of us all. May love of you fill all our senses. May we know no other love except you who are eternal, a love so great that the many waters of these heavens and land and sea will fail to quench it, as is written: 'And many waters could not quench love.' May this be fulfilled also in our case, at least in part, by your gift, our Lord Jesus Christ, to whom be glory for ever and ever. Amen.

IV.

POETRY

Five poems attributed to Columban are accepted by Walker as genuinely his; a sixth – a short epigram on women – is treated as doubtful. They vary in length from the short acrostic poem of seventeen lines to Hunaldus, to the charming poem of almost 160 short lines (with an epilogue added for good measure) to Fidolius. There is a strong didactic strain in all these poems and they are full of such typical Columbanian themes as the shortness of life and the uselessness of worldly things. The three poems to Hunaldus, Sethus and Fidolius have to a great extent the same MS tradition, and a late eighth century MS now in Berlin gives the poet's name as Columbanus. The manuscript evidence for Columban's authorship of De Mundi Transitu *is weak, the poem itself occurring in a Zurich MS of the ninth or tenth century with Columban's name added in the margin by a later hand. The* Carmen Navale *is found only in a tenth-century Leyden MS, where the author's name, partly illegible, is given as '… banus'.*

In view of the above it is not surprising that Columban's authorship of some or all of these poems has been occasionally challenged; most recently and seriously by the Dutch scholar J.W. Smit. His main arguments are as follows:

The author of the prose letters invariably calls himself Columba; the author of the two poems to Hunaldus and to Sethus calls himself Columbanus.

The poetry contains several direct borrowings from classical poets, in sharp contrast to Columban's prose letters, where all the echoes of the classical writers can, in Smit's view, be explained as borrowings from the Fathers, especially from St Jerome.

The classical metres in some of the poetry would make Columban the first Irish author to have used such metres, centuries earlier than any of his fellow countrymen.

Regarding individual poems Smit makes the following points: Hunaldus is a Germanic name which occurs in the eighth century and Sethus might possibly be based on an Arabic name of the ninth century; the rhyme of De Mundi Transitu seems seventh century; acrostics are rare in the sixth century but common in the eighth to ninth centuries; the Fidolio poem uses words used by Alcuin in the ninth century; the '...banus' (author of the Carmen Navale) could be expanded into other names apart from Columbanus.

Smit would therefore reject Columban's authorship of all these poems. The three poems to Hunaldus, Sethus and Fidolius were, in his view, written by an Irishman named Columbanus on the continent during the second half of the ninth century. It may be added that Smit's theory has serious implications for the supposed cultivation of classical literature in the early Irish schools, as Columban's poetry seemed the one irrefutable piece of evidence for this, going back to the sixth century.

In a long scholarly review of Smit's books in Latomus, Vol. 31 (1972), pp. 896–901, Professor Ludwig Bieler pinpoints the inconclusiveness of some of the arguments mentioned above. The absence of direct borrowings from classical authors in Columban's prose writings he would attribute to their style and purpose – written about urgent personal or *ecclesiastical problems, they did not offer the same scope for reflecting on the 'wisdom of the ancients' as did moralising poems. As regards the double name he accepts both Jonas's statement that Columbanus was also known as Columba and the biographer's indiscriminate use of two forms at its face value, and would thus hold that any argument against the authenticity of the Columbanus poems based on the name alone carries no weight. Dr Bieler's overall verdict on Smit's theory is, therefore, that despite the merits of the book, its thesis is unproven.*

It seems likely that Smit's book will provoke much further controversy regarding Columban's writings and especially regarding the poetry attributed to him. Until a consensus emerges among those best qualified to judge, the question must be left open, and this means accepting for the present at least the possibility that Columban may have composed some of the verses which have been attributed to him. We therefore provide a few samples of this work; his claim to the Carmen Navale *is obviously weaker than to the other two pieces given here.*

1. Ad Hunaldum

Hunaldus was in Walker's opinion probably a pupil of Columban – perhaps he studied under Columban in the monastic school of Bangor. This would suggest that the poem belongs to Columban's early life and was written before he left Ireland. At that time his duties as a teacher would have immersed him in Latin studies and there are many echoes of the Latin poets in these lines, one having been directly from Horace, one from Prudentius and one from Juvencus. Two others of the saint's poems Ad Sethum *and* De Mundi Transitu *have also been attributed to his Irish period – in fact Walker*

aptly suggests, because of the rhythm of the latter, tha
written for singing.

The poem Ad Hunaldum *is written in the form of an
acrostic, the initial letters of the lines forming the phrase
'Columbanus Hunaldo'. This was, of course, a literary
device which remained popular with Gaelic poets down to
the eighteenth century. It is one of the two occasions in his
writings when the saint uses the form 'Columbanus'; in his
prose epistles he invariably uses the form 'Columba' and
often plays on the meaning of the name.*

*The poem, as is usual with Columban's writings, stresses
the transitory nature of life, the vanity of earthly glory and
the onrush of eternity. In line 16 the poet seems to realise that
loquaciousness is one of his faults and in line 17 he stresses
the virtue of moderation, something which his critics never
associated with him. In attempting an English translation I
have broken the poem up into short verses.*

Casibus innumeris decurrunt tempora vitae,
Omnia praetereunt, menses volvuntur in annis;
Labitur in senium momentis omnibus aetas.
Ut tibi perpetuam liceat conpraendere vitam,
Molles inlecebras vitae nunc sperne caducae.
Blanda luxuria virtus superatur honesta.
Ardet avaritia caecaque cupidine pectus.
Nescit habere modum vanis mens dedita curis.
Vilius argentum est auro, virtutibus aurum.
Summa quies, nil velle super quam postulat usus.

Hos ego versiculos misi tibi saepe legendos;
Ut mea dicta tuis admittas auribus, oro.
Ne te decipiat vana et peritura voluptas.

Aspice, quam brevis est procerum regumque potestas.
Lubrica mortalis cito transit gloria vitae.
Da veniam dictis, fuimus fortasse loquaces.
Omne quod est nimium semper vitare memento.

Acrostic verses to Hunaldus

In countless ways life's seasons disappear,
They all pass by, the months complete a year,
With every moment, tottering age draws near.

Into eternal life that you may go,
Spurn now the sweet deceits of life below,
Soft lust can upright virtue overthrow.

No breast to blind desire and greed is cold,
A mind rapt up in cares can't judge a deed,
To gold all silver yields, to virtue gold,
The highest peace is but to seek one's need.

This trifling poem I've sent you; read it oft,
Give entrance in your ears to these my words,
Let not some whim seduce you, transient, soft,
See how the power is brief of kings and lords;

Quickly the fame of mortal life is gone;
Pardon my words, perhaps they're overdone:
Whatever is too much, remember, shun!

2. Carmen Navale

This is the most famous of the poems which have been attributed to Columban and one which has deservedly found a place in many anthologies. The reference to the Rhine in line 2 suggested that it was composed by the saint while on his journey up the river in 610, and indeed it was possibly chanted by his monks as they rowed their boat against the flow of water.

It is made up of twenty-four hexameters. A refrain is repeated after every two lines and the refrain itself changes half-way through the poem. In striving to put a rowing movement into the English version I have shortened the lines somewhat and this has meant omitting an occasional word of the original, but I hope I have preserved enough to give the reader some idea of its strength and movement.

En silvis caesa fluctu meat acta carina
Bicornis Hreni et pelagus perlabitur uncta.
Heia viri! nostrum reboans echo sonnet heia!
Extollunt venti flatus, nocet horridus imber,
Sed vis apta virum superat sternitque procellam.
Heia viri! nostrum reboans echo sonnet heia!
Nam caedunt nimbi studio, caeditque procella,
Cuncta domat nisus, labor improbus omnia vincit.
Heia viri! nostrum reboans echo sonnet heia!
Durante et vosmet rebus servate secundis,
O passi graviora, dabit dues his quoque finem.
Heia viri! nostrum reboans echo sonet heia!
Sic inimicus agit invisus corda fatigans,
Ac male temptando quatit intima corda furore.
Vestra, viri, Christum, memorans mens personet heia!
State animo fixi, hostisque spernite strofas,
Virtutum vosmet armis defendite rite.
Vestra, viri, Christum, memorans mens personet heia!
Firma fides cuncta superat studiumque beatum,
Hostis et antiquus cedens sua spicula frangit,

Vestra, viri, Christum, memorans mens personet heia!
Rex quoque virtutum, rerum fons, summa potestas,
Certanti spondet, vincenti praemia donat.
Vestra, viri, *Christum, memorans mens personet heia!*

Boat song

Lo, little bark on twin-horned Rhine
From forests hewn to skim the brine,
    Heave, lads, and let the echoes ring;

The tempests howl, the storm dismay,
But manly strength can win the day,
    Heave, lads, and let the echoes ring.

For clouds and squalls will soon pass on,
And victory lie with work well done,
    Heave, lads, and let the echoes ring.

Hold fast! survive! and all is well,
God sent you worse, he'll calm this swell,
    Heave, lads, and let the echoes ring.

So Satan acts to tire the brain,
And by temptation souls are slain,
    Think, lads, of Christ and echo him.

Stand firm in mind 'gainst Satan's guile,
Protect yourselves with virtue's foil,
    Think, lads, of Christ and echo him.

Strong faith and zeal will victory gain,
The old foe breaks his lance in vain,
    Think, lads, of Christ and echo him.

The King of virtues vowed a prize
For him who wins, for him who tries,
    Think, lads, of Christ and echo him.

3. Fidolio

This poem shows its author in lighter mood and the overall effect is very attractive. The tripping Adonic metre gives an airiness and grace to the poem which at least one critic felt to be so much out of character with the saint that he rejected his authorship of it for this reason alone. However, the content is serious enough – the evil results of wealth as shown by examples borrowed from classical mythology. Most of them are taken from Horace, Odes III, but Virgil and Ovid have also been tapped. Fidolius has not been identified. On the analogy of Sedulius (= Siadal), it may be suggested that he was an Irishman bearing the well-attested name Fiadal.

After 159 versus in Adonic metre, the poem concludes with six lines in hexameter. One of these refers to the writer's age, and while its proper interpretation has given rise to much controversy, it seems to imply that its author is an old man. Walker suggests that the poem may have been composed in Milan in 613 and praises it highly as Columban's most successful literary effort: 'Despite its serious touches, the poem is intensely pleasing; a remarkable production for any author of the sixth century; from the literary point of view, it forms the crown of Columban's achievement', and again 'Latin verses of this quality had seldom been written for 500 years, and it seemed almost that Horace sang again by the lips of an Irish exile in the valley of the Po.'

Only some lines from the beginning of the poem and from the conclusion of the Adonic portion are translated here. I have attempted to carry over some of the lightness of the original into the English version by putting this, too, into short lines of five syllables each.

Accipe, quaeso,
Nunc bipedali
Condita versu
Carminulorum
Munera parva;
Turque frequenter
Mutua nobis
Obsequiorum
Debita redde.
Nam velut aestu
Flantibus austris
Arida gaudent
Imbribus arva,

Sic tua nostras
Missa frequenter
Laetificabat
Pagina mentes
Non ego posco
Nunc periturae
Munera gazae,
Non quod avarus
Semper egendo
Congregat aurum,
Quod sapientum
Lumina caecat
Et velut ignis
Flamma perurit
Improba corda.

Sic tibi Christus,
Arbiter orbis,

Omnipotentis
Unica proles,
Dulcia vitae
Gaudia reddat,
Qui sine fine
Nomine patris
Cuncta gubernans
Regnat in aevum.

To Fidolius
Kindly accept these
Gifts for your pleasure
Written in two-foot
Verse for good measure.

And let you often
Address me a line,
Paying me back too
The due that is mine.
Just as in summer,
When south winds blow high
Showers bring gladness
To fields that are dry.

So with your letter –
From many a start
It reached me at last
And gladdened my heart.
I ask no rich gifts
That will not endure –
Gold that the miser
Hoards up, yet is poor.

It blinds wise men's eyes
And just like the dart
Of a fire, it consumes
The reprobate heart.

Christ be your portion,
Lord of creation,
God the Almighty's
One generation.

May he repay you
With life's sweetest joy
Who, in the name of
His Father on high,
Will govern all things
And rule them for aye.

PART 3

REMEMBRANCE

I.

WHERE COLUMBAN
LABOURED

Fourteen hundred years is, by any standards, a remarkably long time for the memory of a man to remain undimmed. Where the Irish pilgrim sets out in search of St Columban today, he will naturally head first of all for the two great monastic centres associated with his name – Luxeuil and Bobbio. But he should not omit the lesser centres of Columbanian interest – Bregenz which would probably hold his tomb today if a battle had gone the other way, St Gallen where the disciple's cult inevitably preserved the memory of his master, and the numerous villages throughout France and Italy which still bear Columban's name.

Here follows a personal account of one man's visit to these places in search of Columban. The 'pilgrimage' was a thing of bits and pieces, carried out at intervals over several years. It had to confine itself to the big names on Columban's map of Europe, leaving the little places unexplored. But for the sake of completeness it is followed here by some account of the cult of St Columban elsewhere throughout Western Europe, based on the visits and writings of others.

1. Luxeuil, Annegray, Fontaine
Luxeuil-les-Bains, to give it its official name, was easily reached in the past by rail from many directions – from Paris-Est, with a change at Vesoul or Lure, from Basle and Strasbourg via

Belfort and Lure with a change at the latter station, from Belgium and North-Eastern France via Nancy. It is almost 230 miles (366 km) south-east of Paris and visitors by road should take Route Nationale 19 to Chaumont and continue by road 417 via Bourbonne. This route, incidentally, passes through Colombey les Deux Eglises, residence and burial place of the late General de Gaulle.

The present Basilica of Sts Peter and Paul (raised to the rank of basilica in 1926) is the former abbey church, and as far as can be ascertained stands on the actual site of St Columban's first church. The present church is the fourth built on the site and was completed in 1330 by Abbot Eudes de Charenton. It was consecrated on 7 December 1340. Inevitably it has undergone many modifications since then, but basically it is still the same Gothic building after six centuries. Restoration work was carried out by Viollet-le-Duc in the nineteenth century. A porch and window in the south aisle preserve the Romanesque features of the earlier church.

Externally the building is not particularly imposing. Linked up with the adjoining buildings it is impossible to get a good view of the outside of the church as an architectural unit. What was formerly the main doorway was blocked by the construction of the sixteenth-century abbatial palace, and entrance to the church is nowadays obtained through two side doors. The abbatial palace is now used partly as a presbytery and partly as municipal offices.

The interior of the church, on the other hand, impresses the visitor by the majesty and length of its nave. The nineteenth-century stained glass in the apse depicts scenes from the life of St Columban and the 'forty saints of Luxeuil'. Beginning on the left of the apse we have St Columban teaching his Rule to his companions, then miraculously multiplying the corn, being followed by St Lua, and taming wild animals. In the fifth scene Columban the Younger speaks to the birds who nestle in his hood; in the eleventh Gall prays in his retreat in the middle of the forest, in the thirteenth Deicola receives the Papal Bull. The chapel of St Peter in the north transept contains an ancient wooden reliquary in which relics of the saint were formerly preserved.

Not far from the entrance to the church is the remarkable statue of St Columban by Claude Grange erected in 1947. A model of this statue had been exhibited by the sculptor at the Paris Salon in 1935 and awarded the Medal of Honour. The saint is depicted in one of his angry moments as he denounces the immoral life of King Theuderich. It is a sculpture of great power and realism, full of movement and historically accurate, showing the saint wearing a cloak and tunic of rough undyed wool, with his 'Irish' tonsure, his book-satchel slung across his shoulder and his short staff or cambutta in his left hand. Having been blessed and unveiled on 6 July 1947 together with a new bell bearing the name and effigy of the saint, it was inaugurated on 23 July 1950 in the presence of a distinguished gathering which included Pope John XXIII, then Papal Nuncio to France, President de Valera, then leader of Fianna Fáil, John A. Costello, then Taoiseach, Seán MacBride, then Minister for External Affairs, and more than twenty thousand spectators.

A great part of the ancient cloister of the abbey is still preserved and is a splendid example of mainly fifteenth-century work. Some few doorways, windows and underground passages of the medieval monastery also remain, but the bulk of the monastic buildings which exist today are the result of a complete rebuilding of the monastery which was carried out during the seventeenth century under the influence of the Benedictine Reform directed by the Abbey of Saint-Vanne. Its splendid stairways, halls and ceilings make it an interesting example of French seventeenth-century architecture, but it is far removed in spirit from the days of St Columban. The last abbot quit the monastery in 1790, but in 1815 Louis XVIII decreed that the monastic buildings should be used as a minor seminary. They are still employed for this purpose today under the patronage of St Columban.

In the entrance court of the seminary (which was formerly the entrance court of guests to the monastery) a fine bronze statue of St Columban on a tall plinth dominates the surrounding square. Bearing a staff in his left hand and with his right arm outstretched he marches forward courageously into the unknown. The statue was the work of Eugène Traut of Belfort and was erected by the past pupils of the school. It was dedicated by Archbishop Dubourg of Besançon on 20 July 1939. Because of its classification as a work of art it was not melted down under the German occupation, and a long inscription on the plague which now stands before it pays tribute to Columban as the *Apôtre à l'âme de feu, infatigable marcheur à l'étoile* and *sauveur de la civilisation.*

These two modern statues of the saint may be contrasted with some other statues which are still preserved in Luxeuil. One is a seventeenth-century wooden statue in the basilica (the oldest existing statue of the saint in Luxeuil) which shows him dressed in monk's habit with the episcopal mitre at his feet; another in the seminary chapel by the Lorraine sculptor Malet shows the sun on his breast, harking back to Jonas's account of the vision seen by his mother before his birth. The latter is one of a whole series of statues with which Malet decorated the walls of the seminary chapel before the First World War; the saint is, of course, also portrayed in the stained glass windows of the same chapel.

Most of the treasures of the ancient abbey and its library disappeared at the time of the French Revolution. They included relics of St Columban which had been brought from Bobbio, a silver statuette of the saint and many irreplaceable manuscripts in the library. The library was sacked on 22 July 1789 by a mob which seems to have thought that in burning the manuscripts it was destroying the feudal title-deeds whereby most of the peasants still remained serfs on the monastic lands. Some precious manuscripts escaped the general destruction and at least five of these (including the famous seventh-century Gallican Lectionary) are now preserved in the Bibliothèque Nationale in Paris and four others, including a ninth-century Scripture commentary by the Irish scholar Smaragdus, in the British Library in London.

Only one manuscript, formerly in the library of Luxeuil, which contains material in the Irish language, has been preserved. It is a single sheet of parchment which had been used for binding another book. The latter is now Codex 59 in Nancy Library, and the earlier fragment, written in an Irish hand of the ninth century, is attached to its inner cover. It contains Latin notes for calculating the day of the week on which 1 January fell, the age of the moon on 1 January and so on. Interspersed through the Latin notes are six explanatory glosses in Irish, such as *Do toscelad cid lae sechtmaine fora mbí Kl. Jan., Do toscelad cid aes n-escaí bíss for Kl. Jan.* (To ascertain on what day of the week 1 January is; to ascertain what is the age of the moon on 1 January.)

It was only in the twentieth century that the loss of St Columban's relics which Luxeuil suffered at the time of the French Revolution was made good again. On 3 September 1923 new relics of the saint which had come all the way from Bobbio were brought to Luxeuil and on 20 July 1924 they were solemnly enshrined in the basilica in a finely carved wooden shrine surmounted by a replica of Malet's statue of the saint. On 23 July 1950 a relic of St Gall in the form of an arm, which had been brought from St Gallen, was also placed among the basilica's treasures. The anniversary of the return of St Columban's relics has been celebrated annually in Luxeuil since 1924.

To reach the site of St Columban's first foundation at Annegray and the other places in that neighbourhood associated with the saint, one should leave Luxeuil by the Rue des Vosges and pass the villages of Corvereine and Raddon and the ancient Celtic tumulus of Amage. Next comes the village of Ste-Marie-en-Chanois (St Mary's in the Oakwood) and at the further end of the village a path on the left (requiring about half an hour) leads up the hillside to the chapel, cave and holy well of St Columban.

This is the spot traditionally pointed out as the retreat to which the saint used to retire periodically to be alone with God. The bilberry plant which grows wild along the path is still called the *brin belu de St Columban*, and local tradition recalls that when weak with long periods of fasting he was restored by eating the crimson berries. The path finally leads to a ravine, and there one can see the remote cave surrounded by rocks which served as the saint's cell.

To the right of the cave is the holy well, a spring of clear water in the cleft rock which the saint is said to have miraculously caused to gush forth to satisfy his faithful servant Domoal. Some of the country people still come to fetch the healing waters for the sick. The little chapel of St Columban (eleventh century), which stands beside the cave and well, commemorates the expulsion of the bear from the cave and the sudden gushing forth of the spring. The whole site was purchased in 1956 by the Association Internationale des Amis de St Columban.

From the village of Ste-Marie-en-Chanois it is only a short distance to the village of Annegray, picturesquely situated in the valley below, about eight miles east of Luxeuil. When Margaret Stokes visited the village in 1893 she could find no trace of the old church which stood on a round knoll, then a ploughed field, at the foot of a hill overlooking the ancient church of St Martin, not far from the River Breuchin.

However, she found that round the base of the knoll portions of an ancient wall, built of unhewn stone without mortar, and probably part of the original monastic *caiseal* or enclosure, were still standing. The church had been destroyed at the time of the French Revolution. Numerous sarcophagi had been discovered when ploughing the field, but only one was preserved intact, and served as a drinking trough beside the village well! She was told by the local people that 'bones were found everywhere about'.

Since then the site of the monastery at Annegray has been purchased by the Association Internationale des Amis de St Columban and excavations were begun in 1958. The first summer's excavations revealed part of the base of the walls of the church and some stone coffins of the seventh century.

An old building near the site was converted into an oratory and was dedicated to St Columban on 26 July 1959. Pontifical High Mass was celebrated at a temporary alter erected in the open air; Archbishop Dubois of Besançon presided, Bishop Hassler of St Gallen was celebrant and the attendance included Bishop Zuccerino of Bobbio, the Abbot of Bregenz and Mr W.P. Fay, Irish Ambassador to France.

On the same occasion Mr Fay unveiled in Annegray a bust of Mgr Henri Thiébaut (*ob.* 1957), for many years Curé-

Doyen of Luxeuil (1921/47), who did more than anyone in the twentieth century to promote the culture of St Columban. He was the great driving-force behind the international commemoration of St Columban in Luxeuil in 1950, and it was fitting that the National University of Ireland should have conferred the Honorary Degree of LLD on him in recognition of his work in 1951. He had already been decorated by the French Government with the Cross of the Legion d'honneur in 1947.

Fontaine, the site of Columban's third monastery in the Luxeuil area, is only about three miles north-west of Luxeuil. The road leads through the magnificent forests of the Sept-Chevaux. The village is situated on a little rise in the middle of low-lying and formerly marshy country – the tall spire of its parish church is therefore a well-known landmark.

The priory of St Pancras, probably on the site of Columban's foundation, is a completely modern structure which was confiscated under the anti-clerical laws at the beginning of this century. In the stained glass of the east window of the parish church the saint is represented holding the plan of his church in one light and directing the draining of the marshes in another. A modern painting in the church shows him in front of the priory of Fontaine, holding in his hand a scroll bearing the words of Jonas: *Locum quaesit, aliudque monasterium construit, cui Fontanas nomen indidit.* A modern statue of Columban by Grange, the sculptor of the statue of the saint near the door of Luxeuil basilica, was erected in Fontaine in 1950. The parish church also possesses a relic of the saint.

The date of 14 August 1960 is that jotted down in my notes for my first visit to Luxeuil. In some ways it was a disappointment. The enthusiasm inspired by the great international gathering of 1950 seemed to have waned. Mgr Thiébaut was dead, the students of the Petit Séminaire were on vacation, and the basilica and ancient monastic buildings seemed deserted. Even the shops of the town gave little prominence among their picture-postcards to Columbanian associations – while they featured the basilica, the cloisters and the Grange statue, there was no representations of the statues by Traut and Malet, and no views of Annegray or Fontaine. It was difficult to find anyone who knew much about the excavations at Annegray. I now realise, of course, that I should first have addressed myself to someone like Dr Gilles Cugnier, for many years Secretary General of the Friends of St Columban, on whom the mantle of Mgr Thiébaut had fallen. As long as such dedicated disciples of Columban remain in Luxeuil, there is no likelihood that it will be allowed to forget the man who made its name famous throughout Europe.

2. Bregenz

Bregenz is pleasantly situated in the south-eastern corner of Lake Constance where several nations meet. The town itself is in Austria, precariously balanced on the narrow corridor by which Austria reaches the lake, but the German frontier is less than four miles away, Switzerland is five miles to the south-west and Liechtenstein is twenty-four miles to the south. Just south of the town is the high wooded hill of the Gebhardsberg, and the houses in the suburbs go far up the sides of the hill. The town is now a well-known tourist centre for visitors to the Bodensee and Vorarlberg areas.

The original Brigantium, however, was a Celtic settlement which ultimately became an important trading-post and military station of the Roman Empire. In the middle ages it was the seat of the Counts of Bregenz and Montfort and became a Habsburg possession in the sixteenth century. When

Columban arrived in the town towards the end of 610 it had not yet recovered from the Empire's overthrow.

Historians are still somewhat doubtful as to the exact site of the church of St Aurelia, which became the heart of the new Irish monastery. It has been suggested that it was situated in the Olrain area of the city – the present St Gallusstrasse is still in the same area. But it is hard to reconcile this with Walafrid's account of St Gall throwing the pagan idols into the lake, as Olrain is upwards of a mile from the lake shore. What is certain is that this area to the south of the old city has been unbrokenly associated with St Gall (and thereby with St Columban) from the middle ages until the present day.

A rock in this area got the name of Gallusstein (St Gall's Rock) and some markings on it used to be pointed out as the marks of his knees! Here a small chapel arose which was usually referred to as the Gallussteinkapelle. It was certainly there in 1610, a thousand years after the arrival of Gall and Columban. The chapel was allowed to crumble in the nineteenth century and only some fragments of its walls now survive. A short distance north of where it stood, however, the Gallusstrasse (St Gall's Street) still leads north-east into the Kirchstrasse. One of the streets opening into the former from the south-east is the Kolumbanstrasse and this leads to the parish church of the area which is still called St Gallus. It is mentioned as early as the eleventh century and is regarded as perhaps the most beautiful church in Bregenz. Its broad tower in a strikingly unusual style makes it a landmark in the area and its interior baroque decoration is a fine example of the work of the Vorarlberg school.

The St Gallus church was excavated and restored at the beginning of the 1970s, and some remains of a late Roman edifice were discovered under the choir of the present church.

To the west of this, the remains of two early medieval structures came to light. Some scholars have therefore suggested that these late Roman walls marked the site of the fifth-century Church of St Aurelia, which was later restored and extended by the Irish monks. If this interpretation is correct, the parish church of St Gallus was founded on the site of the Irish monastery.

The parish church is first mentioned in 1079. It was then a rectangular building in early Romanesque style, and was later extended and then burnt down in 1477. The present solid Gothic tower was erected after the fire. The frescos were painted by Joseph Ignaz Wegscheider in 1738, and the four statues on the high altar (including St Gall with the bear and log of wood) were sculpted by Johann Georg Brem from Kempten. Another St Gall by Wegscheider appears on the choir-stalls and there is a third St Gall in St Michael's chapel (not accessible). Surprisingly enough, I could not find any paintings or sculptures of St Columban in the church.

By following the Gallusstrasse in the opposite (south-western) direction and continuing along the Landstrasse into which it runs, one comes to the splendid modern church dedicated to St Columban. This building was recently erected and is a fine example of modern religious architecture at its best. The bell-tower is separate from the church building and its striking shape offers an attractive and unusual invitation to the passer-by to visit the Kolumbankirche itself. It was not preceded by an earlier church dedicated to St Columban in this part of the town; hence its interest is aesthetic rather than historical.

In 1985 Bregenz celebrated two thousand years since its foundation (as Brigantium) and St Columban's Church was chosen for the religious ceremonies in connection with the millennium. Its dedicated and learned pastor, Mgr Albert

Holenstein, arranged with the Bishop of Bobbio for the transfer of relics of St Columban to the church in Bregenz and they were solemnly enshrined in a beautiful new reliquary designed and executed by the outstanding German artist, Egino Weinert of Cologne, on the Feast of St Columban, 23 November 1985. A large rock from Bangor was brought to Bregenz for the occasion and was artistically placed on the lawn before the church. The German inscription on it may be translated:

A rock from the sea-coast at Bangor, Ireland. From there came the Irish preacher St Columban as a missionary to the ruined Roman settlement of Brigantium where he preached the Christian faith with God's strength to our forefathers about 610–612 before he proceeded to Bobbio in Italy.

Doctor Patrick Walsh, Auxiliary Bishop of Down and Connor, Fr Gerard Laverty, PP, Bangor and Mgr John Hanly, Rector of the Irish College, Rome, represented the Irish Church at the ceremonies. The church also possesses a fine rugged statue of St Columban.

The millennium led to a twinning arrangement between Bangor and Bregenz. This was placed on an official level at a ceremony in Bangor Town Hall in October 1987, attended by a group from Bregenz including the Burgermeister and the Pastor. It was given a strong religious dimension at a concelebrated Mass in St Comgall's church, Bangor, at which the Auxiliary Bishop of Down and Connor and Mgr Holenstein were concelebrants. The latter, with the approval of Bishop Bruno Wechner of Feldkirch, graciously invited me to administer the sacrament of Confirmation to twenty-two boys and girls of the parish at St Columban at evening Mass in Bregenz on Saturday, 14 May 1988. On the same occasion I had the honour of being invited to sign my name in the Golden Book of the city of Bregenz. St Columban's parish is the missionary centre of the diocese of Feldkirch and missionary bishops from the Third World are often invited to administer Confirmation there. It is in this context the pastor is anxious to build up closer relations with Bangor, training-ground of Bregenz's first great missionary. Thus in 1988 the altar-boys of Bangor and later in the year a group of young people from Bregenz came to Bangor, to stay with local families. Long may this fruitful exchange continue under the patronage of St Columban.

Visitors who are not yet exhausted by the long walk from the Galluskirche to the Kolumbankirche along to Kolumbanstr. and the Gallusstr. (and the Landstr. which follows) should climb further up the steep slopes of the Gebhardsberg until they come to the Gallusstift. This fine building was opened as a Benedictine monastery in 1906 by a group of monks whose monastery at Mariastein in Switzerland had been secularised. A small castle already on the spot became the nucleus of the new monastery and beside it the monks built their new church and monastic buildings. They had wished to build the new monastery further north at the spot where the Gallussteinkapelle had previously stood, but the urban authorities were unwilling to grant them this site. What the monastery lost in historical continuity, however, it gained in scenic surroundings, with the city and the Bodensee opening out below, and high above it, another castle poised perilously on the top of a sheer cliff-face.

During the short period of its existence as a Benedictine monastery (1906–41) most of the monks in the St Gallusstift were of Swiss origin. This provided the excuse for their expulsion during the Hitler regime – in 1941 the majority of the monks were sent back to Switzerland where they returned to Mariastein, and the short career of the St Gallusstift as a Benedictine monastery effectively came to an end. The buildings then came to be used as a secondary school for girls, and they are now the regional library.

The Benedictine connection was not entirely broken, however. One member of the former community, Fr Josef Ketterer, who escaped expulsion because of his German nationality but had to serve in the German army during the war, lived on the St Gallusstift and did parish work in Bregenz. He kindly showed me over the church and monastic buildings on 22 August 1973. The church is tastefully decorated in modern baroque style. One notices immediately on the Gospel side a fine painting of St Gall and his companions preaching the Gospel in the area. It is by the well-known German painter Feuerstein and shows the saint with a mallet in his left hand after having overthrown the pagan idols. With the Bodensee in the background the cross of Christ has been erected over the pagan altar and the idols lie strewn at his feet. The local people gather around the saint to hear the Gospel. Beside him stands Columban, a tall bearded figure dressed in monastic habit and carrying a crozier. One hopes that this church dedicated to St Gall may one day echo again to the chant of the monks.

Some reference must be made to one further monastic establishment in Bregenz where the memory of Columban and Gall is still highly treasured. It is the Cistercian abbey of Mehrerau, delightfully situated near the lake and not far from the yacht-harbour in the north-western suburbs of the town. Of the many monasteries which studded the whole Bodensee area in the past, Mehrerau is the only one which continues as a monastery today.

It was founded as a Benedictine abbey in 1097 and its twelfth-century Romanesque church became the burial place of the Counts of Bregenz and later of the Counts of Montfort. For over seven hundred years it was an important centre of religious life in the Bodensee area. Its Romanesque church was replaced in the eighteenth century by a baroque edifice on the same site and the monastic buildings were re-erected in baroque style. But it finally fell a victim to the secularism of 1806. Its church and tower were pulled down and the stones used to build Lindau harbour.

Half a century later the Cistercians who had been expelled from Wettingen in Switzerland found a refuge here in 1854 with the approval of Emperor Francis Joseph. They erected a new church in neo-Romanesque style in 1855–59. Its simple and well-lighted interior now combines Cistercian austerity with a modernistic twentieth-century atmosphere. Some parts of the monastic buildings, however, have preserved their eighteenth-century baroque ceilings, while the excavations of 1962 have brought many remains of the twelfth-century Romanesque church to light under the present building.

Apart from their spiritual work the monks conduct a well-known boarding school for boys, the Kollegium Sti Bernardi, which is attended by pupils from Austria, Germany and Switzerland. An agricultural school and a convalescent home are also attached to the abbey. But perhaps Mehrerau's greatest achievement during the past century has been the foundation of so many daughter-houses; as a result of this the Cistercians were able to return from Mehrerau to Germany and Switzerland after their nineteenth-century expulsion. In fact the Mehrerau congregation of Cistercians today numbers almost twenty houses.

The prior of Mehrerau at present bears the appropriate name of Dr Kolumban Spahr. From the 1950s on he published many articles on the history and artistic treasures of Mehrerau and of other monasteries associated with it. To his kindness and hospitality I am indebted for the opportunity to see around the monastic building and to learn at first hand of the veneration in which the Irish monks are still held in Mehrerau.

The walls of the monastic cloister were formerly decorated with frescos depicting scenes from the lives of St Boniface and St Columban. Unfortunately these have now disappeared but Fr Kolumban was able to show me a collection of drawings of them in the ninety-thousand-volume library which, besides many manuscripts and incunabula, contains most of the standard works on Columban. The feast-day of the Irish saint is celebrated annually in the monastery. An old painting (recently restored) in the abbey which depicts SS Columban, Gall and Magnus as founders of monastic life in the area, and shows the succession of later abbots from the parent stock, serves to remind the community of the Irish influence on the spread of monasticism in this area.

3. St Gallen

The city called after St Columban's best-known disciple is today a city of eighty thousand people, situated where the plain that stretches south of Lake Constance, from Rorschach inland, begins to rise in a series of medium-sized hills that lead ultimately to the eight-thousand-foot high Santis massif. It is a gay and lively city, the capital of the Swiss textile industry, specialising in linen from medieval times until the eighteenth century and turning since then to cotton and more modern fabrics with equal success. Outside religious and Irish circles it is today the enchanting St Gallen embroideries which make the name of the city well known throughout the world. About 54 per cent of the population are Catholics.

As a city which has mercifully survived without damage in all recent wars it preserves a great number of its historical buildings intact, and a ramble through the streets of the old city with its period houses, famous especially for their outstanding oriel windows, brings one back over the centuries.

The Irish visitor to St Gallen will be particularly interested in the cathedral and library, and the description given here of things of Irish interest in these two places is based on visits to the city at Easter 1952 and in summer 1960, brought up to date by further visits in 1973, 1978, 1980 and 1987.

The cathedral is, of course, the former abbey church, built on the very site, then in the heart of the forest of Arbon, which was chosen by St Gall for his cell and oratory in 612/3 and where he gathered a group of twelve disciples around him. Recent excavations have revealed that St Gall's first church on this site was of stone, not of wood. After the saint's death his disciples maintained a small monastery on the site. Nearly a century later, in 719, the priest Otmar, who had been educated in Chur, set up on the same spot the Abbey of St Gallen under the rule of St Benedict. Its church was sited where the chancel of the present cathedral stands.

Otmar ruled St Gallen as its first Benedictine abbot until his death in 759. By the ninth century the Abbey had become so famous and its monastic school so well known as a centre of learning that church and monastery had to be increased in size. In fact three churches that arose on the site of the present cathedral, St Gall's Church on the site of the present chancel (837), St Otmar's at the present west end (867), and between the two a two-storey building with St Michael's Chapel on its second floor (867); the crypts of St Gall's and St Otmar's Churches (known nowadays respectively as the crypt of St Columban and the crypt of All Saints) still remain within the present cathedral, the former under the sanctuary and the latter now used as the burial-place of the bishops of St Gallen.

A new chancel was built in the fifteenth century, and in the seventeenth the two-storey central part was removed and the nave of St Gall's Church extended to the west. But a great part of the Carolingian buildings remained until the eighteenth century.

The present outstanding baroque edifice was erected as abbey church between 1750 and 1764. Peter Thumb was architect of the central rotunda and nave; the great Freiburg sculptor, Christian Wenzinger, did the stucco reliefs and sculptures; the brothers Gigl did the stucco decoration; and Josef Wannenmacher painted the frescos between 1764 and 1766. But the internal decoration of the church continued over the next few decades and had not been completed when the abbey was secularised in 1805. At that juncture the church became the mother-church of the newly erected diocese of Chur-St-Gallen. The latter became an independent diocese in 1847. Restoration work on the outside of the cathedral was carried out during the decade 1928–38, and the internal decoration was renewed in 1961–67, so that the visitor to St Gallen today is really seeing the masterpiece at its best.

While the description of all the treasures of the cathedral would require many pages, we shall confine ourselves here to those monuments which serve to perpetuate the memory of the first Irish missionaries. The north door into the central rotunda is marked by four life-sized statues of SS Peter and Paul, Gall and Otmar. All these are the work of Wenzinger, and St Gall is easily recognisable above St Peter on the left as one enters, because he is accompanied as usual by the bear. The southern entrance to the rotunda is marked by statues of four other saints and on this side the gable ornament shows St Gall enthroned.

In the interior, scenes from the life St Gall form a considerable part of the decorative scheme. In the ambulatory under the dome Wenzinger has done eight such scenes in stucco relief, four on either side. Those on the right side (as one faces the sanctuary) show the saint carrying out works of mercy, preaching, celebrating Mass and receiving the king's gift of land. Those on the left show Gall smashing the pagan altar, parting from Columban, healing the ruler's daughter and dying.

Wannenmacher's frescos on the ceiling also give a lot of prominence to St Gall. Those diagonally surrounding the dome depict further scenes from his life, while the section of the nave nearest the dome shows him with the patron saints of other Swiss monasteries. He is also depicted in relief on the wickerwork.

But the most noteworthy of all the memorials of Columban and Gall which St Gallen once possessed are no longer there. St Gall's body was burnt by the followers of Zwingli in 1529 and only relics which had been taken from the main shrine before then have been preserved. Most are now enshrined on St Gall's altar, which is just inside the chancel railing on the Epistle side. The saint's skull is in the chapel of the episcopal residence directly above the St Galluskappelle on the ground floor.

For centuries the staff sent by the dying Columban to Gall was also preserved in the abbey church suspended above the high altar. Notker Balbulus mentions it as being still there at the beginning of the tenth century. He tells the story of how he used the staff to put the devil to flight and in striking at the apparition he broke it.

The staff was later brought to Füssen which had been founded by Gall's disciple Magnus. As described by the Bollandists in their Life of St Magnus, published in 1748, it was three feet long with no crook at the top and had been mounted in a silver shrine with a figure of St Columban on the head. The place where it had been broken was then still visible.

The former monastic buildings of St Gallen are used for diverse purposes today. The buildings around the outer court are now government offices from which the administration of the canton of St Gallen is carried out. The building on the other side of the Church of the Holy Angels is now a school. The buildings around the inner court include ecclesiastical offices and apartments. And on the same side of the cathedral is the library, still housed in the magnificent baroque hall which was built for it when the monks were still in possession of the abbey. Over the entrance portal is the famous inscription *Psychés Iatreion* – translated by Diodorus Siculus from the library erected by King Rameses of Egypt about 1250 BC – which is also inscribed over the public library in Armagh.

The builders and decorators of the church were also responsible for the library. Peter Thumb was architect of the library wing which was built in 1758, the Gigl brothers did the stucco work in the library in 1761/62 and Joseph Wannenmacher painted the frescos on the ceiling (depicting the first four ecumenical councils) in 1762/63. Various brothers in the community made the beautiful bookcases and other furniture. All together have combined to produce what has been described as the finest baroque building of a secular character that exists in Switzerland.

The library now serves as a specialist library for medieval studies, comprising about a hundred thousand volumes which include two thousand manuscripts and 1,650 incunabula. Here we can mention only the manuscripts of particular Irish interest. They include fifteen from the seventh to the twelfth century, which means that St Gallen possesses more manuscripts written by Irishmen or under Irish influence during the pre-Norman period of our history than all the libraries of Ireland together.

Only one of these manuscripts is among the treasures of the library which are on permanent display. It is MS 51, a Latin Gospel-book with twelve full-page miniatures from about 750. The visitor from Ireland will recognise at once the 'Celtic' designs of its carpet page. But three other manuscripts among the fifteen are complete volumes: 1. MS 48: a Greek Gospel-book from about 850; 2. MS 60: a copy of St John's Gospel in Latin with two miniatures from about 800. This manuscript is mentioned in a catalogue of the library made in 847; 3. MS 904: a copy of Priscian's Latin Grammar with glosses in Old Irish from about 850.

The last-mentioned is of course one of the sources which have been used by scholars to reconstruct the grammar of Old Irish, and glosses from it are familiar to all students of Celtic studies. It seems to have been written in a monastic scriptorium in Ireland where the master was named Maelbrighde; the principal scribes were named Maelpádraig and probably Cairbre, and shorter portions were written by Finguine and Donngus. One of the scribes declares that he and Donngus were from Inis Maddoc, which has been identified as the island in Templeport Lake, Co. Leitrim.

The marginalia in this manuscript afford fleeting glimpses into the thoughts of the monastic scribes as they toiled away in the scriptorium – here and there a brief invocation of a saint (St Brigid was particularly popular with them): *Fave Brigita, Sancta Brigita ora pro nobis, Sancta Brigita adiuva scriptorem istius artis ... thas Patric agus Brig – ar Mael Brite na mba olc a meanna frímm ar an scríbheann ro scríobhadh an dul so;* at other times a scrap of conversation often about the ink and parchment, perhaps to bypass the monastic rule of silence: *Beannacht for anmain Feargusa; Is dorcha dom; Do Inis Maddoc dínn .i. mise agus Cairbre; Is gann an meamram agus a scríbheann; Ni ro mhall ro scríobhadh an leatraim so; Uch mo chliabh, a Naomh-inghean; Meadhon lae; Is tana an dubh; Meamram nua, droch-dubh, o ni abraim ni eile.* (Spelling somewhat modernised here.)

The same manuscript contains three or four quatrains of poetry in Irish which would otherwise have been lost to us. These stray fragments include the well-known verse *Is acher an ghaoth anocht* in which the scholar welcomes the howling wind because it will prevent a Viking raid over the sea, and the picturesque description of the scribe's surroundings with a hedge of trees all around and the blackbird and cuckoo singing from the tops of the bushes.

One final indication of the artistry which the monastery of St Gallen employed to perpetrate the memory of its founder must be mentioned. It is the small St Gallus chapel situated on the ground floor of one of the buildings of the inner court.

Abbot Purchart erected the first chapel of St Gall on this spot in 971. According to tradition it marked the place where Gall had first set up the Cross in this area. During the Reformation troubles the chapel was razed to the ground in 1530, but by 1540 a new round chapel had replaced it and was consecrated in that year. Abbot Gallus II laid the foundation stone of the present chapel on this spot on 28 July 1666. It was no longer a free-standing edifice, but was incorporated in the new monastic buildings, with another chapel of St Gall immediately above it, which has served since then as the private chapel of the episcopal residence.

The outstanding feature of the chapel of St Gall on the ground floor is the cycle of twenty-four paintings on light canvas affixed to the walls, depicting scenes from the lives of SS Columban and Gall. There should be twenty-six paintings in the cycle, but paintings 6 and 9 have been missing since the nineteenth century. When the paintings were restored in 1974/5, it was discovered that they were originally painted by Johann Sebastian Hersche in and after 1670 and brilliantly restored by Joseph Wannenmacher about 1760. The latter has already been mentioned for his outstanding frescos in the cathedral and library. Columban appears in paintings 1 (receiving Gall as a boy), 2 (teaching Gall), 3 (being received with Gall by King Sigebert) and 20 (Columban on his death-bed sends his crozier to Gall who offers Mass for his former abbot). None of the paintings shows the dispute between the two Irishmen.

The feast of St Gall is celebrated annually on 16 October with a Pontifical Mass in the cathedral, in which the ecclesiastical and civil authorities participate on a large scale. The present Bishop of St Gallen, Dr Otmar Mäder, kindly invited me to be chief concelebrant of this Mass in 1987. As the Bishops' Synod was in session in Rome at the time and the installation of Dr Joseph Cassidy as Archbishop of Tuam took place on the following Sunday, it was possible to fly from Rome to Zurich and proceed by road to St Gallen before continuing the journey to Ireland. The packed congregation at the Mass and the splendid singing of the St Galler Domchor (Mass in E by Anton Bruckner) added much to the splendour of the occasion.

The former Abbey Library of St Gallen, under the Stiftsbibliothekar, Dr Peter Ochsenbein (successor to Dr Johannes Duft), arranged a series of lectures and discussions on St Gall's life, influence and cult on the eve of the feast-day. Apart from Dr Ochsenbein and his predecessor the participants in the Gallus-Kolloquium include such well-known scholars in these fields as Professor Walter Berschin of Heidelberg, Dr Gerold Hilty of Zurich and Dr Hans Lieb of Schaffhausen. At the Gallus-Kolloquium I learned for the first time that an occasional scholar now questions the Irish origin of St Gall.

4. San Columbano Al Lambro

To represent the numerous towns and villages in France and Italy which are called after the Irish saint, let us select the largest – San Colombano al Lambro, now a town of eight thousand people, situated about twenty kilometres south of Lodi where Napoleon performed one of his most heroic feats at the bridge over the Addo. By taking the main road from Lodi to Pavia as far as San Angelo (13 km) where Mother Cabrini was born, and then turning down the valley of the Lambro as it flows south to join the Po, the visitor will add five or six kilometres to his journey but will be rewarded with some fine views of the river valley. The autostrada from Milan to Piacenza also passes within a short distance of the town.

Near the town a lonely hill covered with vineyards rises over two hundred feet above the surrounding plain. It is the *collina di S. Colombano*, mentioned so affectionately by the seventeenth-century scholar-poet Redi in his *Bacco in Toscana*:

> ... bel colle,
> cui bacia il Lambro il piede
> ed a cui Columbano il nome diede ...

> ... that fair hill
> whose foot the Lambro kisses
> and to which Columban gave his name ...

This verse is put into the mouth of Bacchus – hence the present-day vineyards of San Colombano have a long and distinguished ancestry!

An ancient tradition holds that the Irish saint passed this way on his journey from Milan to Bobbio, and having converted the inhabitants taught them the cultivation of the vine. But the story of an Irishman teaching Italians how to make wine seems a little too 'Irish'! While it is not improbable that the saint may have passed by Piacenza, the well-known Columbanian scholar Don Annibale Maestri has shown in a series of articles published in the 1930s that the name of the town originated in the extensive landed property which the Abbey of Bobbio once possessed in this area. The place is mentioned under its present name at least as early as the eleventh century.

The town possesses an old castle that once belonged to Frederick Barbarossa. It later passed into the hands of the Visconti and has now been restored by the Barbiano family. Its chapel, now demolished, had frescos painted by Bernardino Campi, but these have been transferred to the parish church.

The parish church, a long Romanesque building culminating in a rounded apse and surmounted by a slender tower, is dedicated to St Columban. It was originally built in the tenth century and the round pillars of the first edifice still remain. The church was enlarged in the nineteenth century by the addition of the present sanctuary and apse; and the altar, which in the original building stood where the main door now is, was then moved around to its present position.

On the Epistle side of the high altar is the altar dedicated to St Columban. A sixteenth-century statue of the saint surmounts it, showing him as a bearded man but without the sun on his breast as in so much Columban iconography. On the altar is the shrine of the saint's relics, in the form of a hand and arm not unlike the 'Shine of St Patrick's Hand' in St Malachy's College, Belfast. The shrine contains a tooth and finger-bone of the saint. In the parish is a flourishing confraternity of 'Oblates of St Columban'.

According to some notes jotted down on the occasion, I travelled by bus from Lodi to San Colombano (via St Angelo) on 30 August 1967.

I was fortunate enough to meet a young priest at the door of St Columban's Church who brought me to the parish priest's residence. The latter was delighted to meet a countryman of St Columban – it was flattering to be told that it was the first time since his ordination in 1945 that he had shown an Irishman over the church dedicated to an Irish saint. But then he had spent his whole priestly life teaching Classics in the Diocesan Seminary in Lodi and had been appointed parish priest of St Columban's only three weeks before! Devotion to the saint is still alive in the parish and his feasts are celebrated both on 21 November (for the 23rd, the day of his death?) and on 30 July, the date of the translation of his relics to Bobbio.

5. Bobbio

Bobbio is small, secluded and cheap. It has a bishop, a mayor, a cathedral, a basilica and little more than two thousand inhabitants. One should, I suppose, approach it from Piacenza as Columban did. Coming down from the north in that way it is only forty-eight kilometres from Piacenza, and the countryside along the route is level except for the last few miles. There is a reasonably good bus service, one for every two hours. The diocese is now Piacenza-Bobbio.

It suited me better, however, to approach Bobbio from the south. I had already spent some days in Genoa, hardly conscious at the time of all the Irishmen who had died in that city – Daniel O'Connell in 1847 and Cúchonnacht Mag Uidhir in 1608, not to mention the famous Tyrone Franciscan Fr Mícheál Ó Duibhinn who died there in 1652. I discovered that it was possible to travel all the way from Genoa to Piacenza by a network of buses, one of which could pass Bobbio on the way. This was to be my route. The date entered in my notes is Friday, 25 August 1967.

We left the Piazza della Vittoria at 11.50 a.m. for the town of Ottone. Soon the bus abandoned the flat land across the sea-coast on which the city of Genoa is built and began to climb up the steep river-valley inland. We passed the huge city cemetery with its thousands of elaborate monuments, one of them marking the grave of Giuseppe Mazzini. As the road ascended the steep gradients it twisted and curled like some gigantic serpent asleep on the mountainside. The bus was now reduced almost to walking pace as it puffed and snorted its way around 'S' bends and up corkscrew hills, sometimes only a few feet from the edge of a frightening precipice which afforded an unhindered view into the ravine below. Only later did I discover that Hemingway wrote of this valley as 'the loveliest on earth'. I was so overcome by the grandeur of it all that I scarcely noticed the two hours which it took our expert driver to cover the seventy kilometres as far as Ottone.

After a forty-five-minute break for a midday meal, we were off again on the second stage of our journey. The countryside was similar to the first part, though perhaps a trifle less awe-inspiring, and it changed little until we arrived in Bobbio after another thirty kilometres at about 4.00 p.m.

Bobbio is situated in a wide part of the valley of the Trebbia. An old medieval stone bridge, which looks as if some of its arches could go back almost to Columban's own day, crosses the river with many humps and curves at the edge of town.

Like so many similar bridges in this part of Italy it looked much wider than the river it crossed, for the river-bed, apart from a small stream of water in the centre, was dried up under the hot August sun. But one could easily imagine how in the wintertime, with the streams gushing down from Monte Penice, the Trebbia would be turned into a swirling torrent. The bridge bears a rather crude effigy of St Columban.

Under the expert guidance of Fr Malacalza, parish priest and custodian of the museum, the visit to the Basilica of San Colombano was a rare pleasure. This was of course formerly the abbey church and is now used as a parish church. The oldest parts of the church above the ground are the sanctuary (with its absidioles) and the tower, both of which go back to the tenth or eleventh century. The nave of the church and the adjoining monastic buildings are fifteenth century. A small statue of St Columban stands in the façade above the main door of the church and both sides of the sanctuary are decorated with frescos depicting scenes from his life. They were painted during the latter part of the fifteenth century. On a pedestal behind the high altar is a large statue of the saint holding a book in his hand and with the sun on his breast.

Under the basilica is a crypt at two levels, the lower level beneath the sanctuary. Here is the tomb of St Columban, a white marble sarcophagus with the simple Latin inscription: *Hic quiescit in pace Christi S. Columbanus Abbas* and with scenes from his life carved on three sides by the sculptor Giovanni di Argennio in 1480. Beside the tomb is a modern altar erected early in the present century as a result of a collection taken up in Ireland at the request of Cardinal Logue. The Cardinal's name is still legible in the inscription around the altar. A priest saying Mass at the altar would be gazing at the saint's tomb in front of him – this side of the tomb was left undecorated by the fifteenth-century sculptor, but a harp and some shamrocks have been carved on it in modern times.

Facing the altar is a stained-glass window installed in 1910 depicting the saint, with another window of St Patrick banishing the snakes on his right and on his left a third of St Benedict and the raven. Along the wall opposite the tomb of St Columban are the tombs of his two successors as abbots of Bobbio – Attala (*ob.* 627) and Bertulf (*ob.* 640). On the other side is a very ornate iron grille. The upper level of the crypt contains the famous medieval mosaic showing the signs of the Zodiac. Unfortunately it is now incomplete.

Part of the former monastic building is now used as a school. Another part has been transformed into a museum where many of the treasures of the former abbey are now carefully preserved. Here on show the items known as *La tazza di San Columbano* (St Columban's cup), a wooden vessel from which a young prince of the Lombards drank and was cured of fever; *Il coltello di San Colombano* (St Columban's knife) with its long blade and handle of horn; St Columban's bell; and the famous inscribed stone bearing the name of Cummian which was erected by Liutprand, King of the Lombards, in the early eight century. The museum also houses some medieval shrines made for relics of St Columban and his successors, including a silver bust of the Irishman (depicted as a mitred abbot) which was made to receive a portion of his skull.

Bobbio has several other churches apart from the cathedral and the basilica. There is for instance the confraternity chapel under its low tower at the other end of the monastic cloister from the basilica, the Church of San Lorenzo not far from the basilica and the Church of Nostra Signora del Aiuto (Our Lady of Help), under whose patronage the town was placed some years ago. But none of these is a parish church, that honour being shared with the cathedral only by St Columban's Basilica. On the summit of Monte Penice, nearly five thousand feet high, a new church now stands where its predecessors have stood for a thousand years.

The two grottoes to which, according to tradition, Columban used to retire for silent prayer are still pointed out on the mountainside. That to the north-east of Bobbio is a small cave about five feet long and seven feet high in a steep cliff-face some five hundred feet above the Trebbia valley from which a foaming torrent dashes down into the river below. The place was called La Spanna from an open hand carved on the rock to mark the border of the province of Pavia. The other grotto – to the south-west of Bobbio towards San Salvador – is now a large cave some twenty feet long and eight feet high. In St Columban's days a small oratory dedicated to St Michael stood beside it. According to tradition it was here that Columban died.

Next morning at Mass many thoughts were rambling through my mind – of Columban doing that same journey from Ireland but doing it all on foot, of Cardinal Logue arriving from Armagh in 1906 to find the tomb deserted and the crypt dilapidated, of Sean T. and Dev coming at different times as leaders of the Irish people to the tomb of their greatest exile, of Cardinal Conway's visit on 23 November 1965 to assist at the celebration marking thirteen and a half centuries since Columban's death. The most recent presidential visit took place on 28 October 1989, when President and Mrs Hillery received a tumultuous welcome.

The bus for Piacenza left at 10:35 a.m., keeping to the valley of the Trebbia until it descended into the plain. A few miles outside Bobbio we passed a roadside statue of the saint which marks perhaps the limits of the former abbey lands.

Out there in the undulating countryside, on the road which Columban had traversed in the opposite direction thirteen and a half centuries ago, it was a good place to say goodbye to Columban with the thought that as long as he can inspire such devotion in the country towns and villages of Italy and Ireland, there is still hope of a second spring.

I have returned to Bobbio many times since that first visit. Perhaps the most interesting time was in 1978 when I accompanied a BBC Northern Ireland camera team in the footsteps of St Columban from the English Channel to his tomb in Bobbio. They were a mixed group of Protestants and Catholics, unionists and nationalists, and the director of the film was a Presbyterian clergyman. I noticed then how we all looked back to Columban as a father-figure whom we share. It is no wonder the film was later awarded an Italian prize.

II.

Widespread cult throughout Europe

B **rittany**
According to long-standing Breton tradition the village of
St-Coulomb, beside the Bay of St Malo, is named after the Irish
saint. A granite cross which still bears his name is held to mark
the spot where he first set foot on French soil. The cross, erected
in 1892 overlooking a fine beach about a mile from St-Coulomb
on the coast road from St Malo to Cancale bears an inscription in
French at its foot stating that according to tradition St Columban
began his work of evangelisation here. It stands on top of a cairn
of stones beside a portion of an earlier cross which marked the
site. Visitors are requested to recite a *Pater, Ave* and the *Fidelium
Animae* to gain one hundred days' indulgence. It was customary
in the past, during periods of drought, to pray at this cross for
rain. The village of St-Coulomb now has a statue of the saint,
and the local parish church depicts him in one of its stained-glass
windows, but his annual feast-day is no longer observed.

Near the small town of Miniac-Morvan in the diocese of
Rennes is a marshy swamp known as *la mare St-Colomban*.
Local tradition affirms that the saint passed this way after his
arrival in Gaul and his memory was preserved by the erection
of an oratory in the forest. But the area was later inundated by
the sea and all trace of a local cult has disappeared.

The neighbouring diocese of Saint-Brieuc contains two
well-known centres of Columbanian devotion. Brélidy claims

to possess relics of the saint which are preserved in a very ornate shrine. Twice each year, on 21 November and on the fifth Sunday after Easter, the local 'pardon' in honour of the saint takes place. A special Mass for the sick is celebrated and the pilgrims kiss the shrine. They then go to drink the water of St Columban's well. A fine seventeenth-century wooden statue of the saint stands in St Columban's Church, and the congregation often sing a Breton hymn in his honour.

Plouvénez-Quintin, also in the diocese of Saint-Brieuc, has a very ancient chapel dedicated to the saint which was restored in 1838. Here also some relics of Columban, authenticated by Cardinal Godescalchi in 1837, are exposed for the veneration of the faithful. As at Brélidy, the saint is honoured by a statue, a hymn and a holy well, but the 'pardon' takes place on the Sunday after 24 June.

Passing into the diocese of Vannes we meet the cult of Columban at Carnac and Loyat, both of which have chapels dedicated to him. The chapel in the Carnac neighbourhood, so renowned internationally for its megalithic monuments, is a couple of kilometres west of the town. Follow the street of St Columban towards the sea and St Columban's beach. After passing the emigrants' cross you come to the saint's holy well (La Fontaine de St Colomban) on the left of the road, surrounded by a sixteenth-century shrine. It had a good supply of water, three feet deep, at the time of my last visit. St Columban's Church is not far beyond the well.

At Loyat St Columban's Chapel is the remains of a religious home suppressed during the French Revolution. Occasionally the clergy assemble there to chant vespers in honour of the saint. His memory is recalled in Loyat by a statue and a holy well.

Malansac has a small chapel, of which he is joint patron, outside the town and a large effigy of the saint in the parish church. Locminé was once the site of a monastery founded from Luxeuil, which understandably helped to spread devotion to the saint in this part of Brittany. The present church replaced the monastery in the sixteenth century and contains a Chapel of St Columban on the north side of the nave, with an altar and statue of the saint and some portions of a fifteenth-century window depicting scenes from his life. It was customary in the past for people suffering from nervous troubles to come from afar in order to pray in this chapel, and they were placed in a sort of cell, as in the church of St Dymphna at Gheel (Belgium). The cell was closed during the Napoleonic period and the present-day cult is confined to the parish. The patron day is celebrated here on the last Sunday of June.

In this area of Brittany the name of Columban has been corrupted into various forms which are barely recognisable. He has become St Clomer, St Clomes, St Colombier; in Quiberon he has even become St Clement. For this reason the cult of Pope St Clement has actually supplanted that of Columban in some parts of Brittany!

In the far west of Brittany we reach the diocese of Quimper, where traces of devotion to St Columban can still be found. The former Benedictine Abbey of Sainte-Croix was its promoter. Quimperlé once had a fine parish church dedicated to the saint which is now in ruins, but near the ruins is a modern cinema which now bears his name! Lanmeur formerly had a hospice and Locmaria a monastery dedicated to him, but these have passed away. Kernevel, however, retains him as its patron. The sixteenth-century church which bears his name has one of the oldest statues of the saint now in existence (probably dating from the sixteenth century) and also shows him in its stained glass. On Sundays the faithful sing a Breton hymn in his honour and on the third Sunday of November they celebrate his 'pardon' by a procession of his relics.

La Vendée

The village and parish of St-Colomban, situated in that part of the département of Loire-Inférieure, which is south of the River Loire and near the borders of the modern département of Vendée, preserves the name of the Irish saint in an area which he visited after his expulsion from Luxeuil. The place name is usually spelled with an 'i' in the final syllable. The original church from which it took its name may have been founded in the seventh century by St Philibert (*ob.* 685) or in the ninth century by the monks of Noirmoutier who had to fly from their monastery during the Norman invasion.

Situated in an area which always remained staunchly Catholic, St-Colombin was in the heart of the Vendée resistance to the republic in 1793/94. On 10 February 1794 the village was burned to the ground by the republican forces and almost all its inhabitants were massacred beside the old Church of St Columban.

Côte d'azur

The diocese of Nice contains a village and parish named St-Colomban beside the town of Lantosque (Dép. Alpes-Maritimes). It was once part of the domain of the monks of Lérins, who may have been responsible for bringing the name and fame of the Irish monk to this area.

The present church was built in the seventeenth century to replace an earlier chapel. It claims to possess relics of the saint which were enshrined in a statue of St Columban in 1656 in such a way as to leave them visible. Pilgrims still assemble to honour the relics on the patron day, the first Sunday of September. In this area St Columban is invoked particularly for the cure of sick children.

Savoy

High among the mountains of Savoy is the village and parish of St-Colomban-des-Villars, near the town of St Jean de Maurienne. It is not far from what still remains one of the great traffic arteries between France and Italy, the road and railway from Chambéry to Turin via the Mt Cenis tunnel and on through Susa where Jonas was born. The parish church of the village is dedicated to the Irish saint, but I have not succeeded in tracing the origin of the cult in this area.

Alsace

It seems likely that Columban journeyed through Alsace before proceeding to Switzerland and Austria – indeed when Walafrid Strabo in his Life of St Gall mentions that Columban inserted relics of St Aurelia in the altar of the new church at Bregenz, he leaves it open to us to deduce that the saint had come via Strasbourg where the grave of St Aurelia was. The late seventh century saw the establishment in this region of a number of monasteries which followed the Rule of Columban, and it is probably through these that the cult of the saint was introduced into Alsace.

Church dedications, liturgical calendars, reliquaries, litanies, etc., all bear witness to a widespread devotion to Columban here in the middle ages. It was, however, a liturgical and monastic cult rather than a popular devotion among the people. In the middle ages he became patron of the parish church of Garrebourg, which belonged to the monastery of Maursmünster during the first half of the twelfth century.

Today St Columban still remains patron of this parish church, which belonged to the diocese of Metz after the Napoleonic era. The diocese of Strasbourg has now only one parish church dedicated to the saint, that of Bisel in the Sundgau. It belonged originally to the Abbey of Remiremont which was founded from Luxeuil. The Cathedral of Strasbourg, however, shows Columban among the great founders of religious orders, painted in the choir in 1878 by Eduard von Steinle.

Corsica

Devotion to the saint was once widespread on the island, but it has died out and left few traces except a number of place-names derived from Columban's name. It came to the island in medieval times, of course, via Genoa, which had the closest commercial and political links with Corsica after the overthrow of the Saracens in the eleventh century.

In the north of the island the road from Ponte Leccia to Calvi encounters in turn a stream called the *Rio di S. Colombano*, a pass called the *Passo di S. Colombano*, a hill called the *Monte di S. Colombano* and a ruined castle, the *Torre di S. Colombano*. The latter was built by the papacy in the eleventh century. Another *Castello di S. Colombano* once stood on the site of the present town of Rogliano on the Northern tip of the island, but it was destroyed by the Genoese in 1554 and only a few tenth- or eleventh-century towers remain. Its lord was known as *Sancti Columbani princeps*, and the later descendents of this family took the surname Columbani or Columbo. In fact, it has been suggested that Christopher Columbus, who was born in Genoa, belonged to a family which had moved there from Corsica and took his surname from the Irish saint. With the rapid spread of the Franciscans in Corsica from the thirteenth century on (at one stage they had as many as sixty houses in this small island), devotion to St Francis and the other saints of the order gradually supplanted what remained of the cult of the Irishman. Today not a single church in Corsica is dedicated to him.

Germany

Although Columban's journey across half of Europe brought him up a long stretch of the Rhine, he never penetrated into the heart of what is now Germany. Not surprisingly, the cult of St Columban was not to be found in subsequent centuries as extensively in Germany as in France, Switzerland and Northern Italy. Devotion to St Gall spread northward from St Gallen in the middle ages throughout much of what was then the Holy Roman Empire, and churches dedicated to him are still frequently found in Bavaria and Franconia. A number of holy wells bear his name, and he is also invoked, notably in Bavaria, as a *Speisespender*, a bestower of food. But his master never became an object of popular devotion on German soil to the same extent.

Emperor Henry II (1014–24) had an altar erected in honour of Columban in Bamberg Cathedral. The abbey of Hirschau, in the diocese of Speyer, dedicated an altar in its church to a number of monastic saints, including Columban in 1091. Verses in honour of St Columban are included in the *tituli* which Rabanus Maurus composed for the abbey church of Fulda in the ninth century. Churches or chapels dedicated to the Irish saint were also erected in Ochsenhausen, Weingarten, Wiblingen, Schweiningen and Salem, while relics of him were claimed by Augsburg, Gorse and Goslar. The circumstances which led to the deposition of part of St Columban's cambutta in Füssen have already been explained. The shrine containing it was opened by the Rector of the Jesuit College in 1607 and relics of SS Gall and Eustasius were found inside. It was venerated in the countryside around Füssen as a shield against crop pests. Portions of the cambutta were given to the Canons Regular of Schiessenriedt in Suabia and to the Cistercians of Kempten about 1700.

Colomban's name was attached to some holy wells in Germany, and a prayer in Old German, dating from the sixteenth century, was called *Segen des heiligen Columbanus* (Blessing of St Columban). Some versions of this prayer have substituted the name Coloman for Columban, and it is just possible therefore that the cult of the seventh-century abbot has been swallowed up in some parts of Southern Germany in devotion to the eleventh-century Irish pilgrim-martyr. Churches dedicated to St Coloman or Koloman (who was murdered at Stockerau in 1012 and whose relics rest in Melk) are very common throughout Bavaria today, but I have not come across a single church whose patron is St Columban.

Switzerland

Basle was the first place in modern Switzerland which Columban reached. His feast has been celebrated there for centuries and a fourteenth-century monstrance in the cathedral shows him side by side with its two great benefactors, Emperor Henry and Kunigunde. For centuries too the chapel of St Gall there preserved 'the foot of the innocent child', a relic of the Holy Innocents which allegedly had been donated by Columban himself. In 1470 it was enshrined in a precious reliquary ornamented with jewels and enamels. During the outbreak of iconoclasm in Basle in 1529 it was removed from the cathedral, and the reliquary ultimately came to Paris. The relic was presented to the Abbey of Beinwil-Mariastein in 1833 and remains there today.

From Basle, St Columban and his companions had followed the course of the Rhine and the Aare until they reached the old Roman road that went east past Zurich. The spot where they halted near Tuggen on Lake Zurich and where, according to local tradition, St Gall began preaching to the Alemanni, is still marked by St Gall's well. Tuggen also preserves the memory of Columban. His image is in stained glass in the local church; his feast is celebrated annually with more than usual solemnity and his reliquary is placed on the altar for the occasion; even the town band displays his picture on its banner.

We cannot be certain of the route which the Irish monks took from Tuggen to Arbon – perhaps via Herisau where a cave now called *Sanggeliboo*, a corruption of *Sankt Columba*, is still pointed out as one of the spots where Columban stopped to pray. Nearby, at Flawil, is a spring called *Kolumbansbrünnlein*, St Columban's well. Then the saint crossed by boat from Arbon to Bregenz where the various sites associated with the Irish missionaries have already been listed.

The last stage of Columban's journey – up the Rhine valley to Chur and then across the Alps to Italy – has fewer vestiges nowadays of personal associations with the saint. He may have passed by Wangs, which was once a possession of Bobbio and claimed to have some of his relics. The church in Sagens is dedicated to him, but this was probably due to the influence of the abbey of St Gall. Marienberg on the upper Etsch had relics of the Irishman from the thirteenth century on. Spiez in the Berner Oberland had a church dedicated to him as early as 800 but this was probably due to the influence of Luxeuil.

In Eastern Switzerland the cult of St Gall naturally overshadowed that of his master. Yet the monastery of St Gallen made its own contributions to the cult of St Columban, both in the city itself (which has already been covered) and in the territory south of Lake Constance. Rorschach is only one of the towns in that area today to possess a St Columban's Church. Statues of Columban and Gall flank the high altar and a cruciform reliquary of the former is preserved there. St Columban's feast-day is celebrated annually as the parish patron day.

Through the influence of the Abbey of St Gall, the cult of Columban spread to Uster and Pfäfers. In the case of Andermatt, however, the point of origin was probably the Abbey of Disentis, founded by Columban's disciple Sigebert. Before the year 1000 the church of Andermatt was already dedicated to St Columban. Devotion to the saint remained very strong until the early seventeenth century. The erection of a new parish church in the seventeenth century, dedicated to SS Peter and Paul, caused the Irish saint to recede somewhat into the background, but he made a great come-back from 1733 on, when his church at Andermatt received a reliquary containing a tooth of the saint from the Abbot of Bobbio. The church was renovated in 1942 and continues to draw large numbers of pilgrims. The village of Scona beside the town of Olivone has a little St Columban's chapel which was renovated in 1939. The abbeys of Pfäfers and Einsiedeln claim to possess relics of the saint.

Italy

Inside Italy the cult of St Columban has for centuries been almost exclusively confined to the North. In this area alone forty parishes are dedicated to him apart from chapels, altars and other institutions; besides these his name figures in several place-names. We can deal only with the more important or more interesting examples in what follows.

Piedmont

Between Turin and Viù there is a Monte Colombano rising to a height of five thousand feet. Three villages in this part of Northern Italy bear the name San Colombano – one is part of the commune of Exilles near the French frontier, another is near Gattinara in the province of Vercelli, and the third, called San Colombano Belmonte, is part of the commune of Cuorgnè in the province of Aosta.

Five churches in Piedmont are dedicated to the saint, the most notable being, perhaps, the parish church of Pagno in the diocese of Saluzzo.

Liguria

The valleys stretching inland from the Ligurian coast below Genoa are full of memories of St Columban. Here one finds the parishes of San Columbano di Vignale (parish church from 1142) and San Colombano della Costa (parish church from 1207), both ancient foundations from Bobbio. The thirteenth centenary of the saint was commemorated with great enthusiasm in Vignale in 1920, and crowds gather there annually for the celebration of his feast-day. The dioceses of Luni-Sarzana, Albenga and Acqui have each one parish dedicated to the saint.

Lombardy

Here the most notable centre of Columbanian devotion is the town of San Colombano al Lambro, which has been mentioned above. In addition, the little Romanesque Church of St Columban (eleventh to twelfth centuries) at Vaprio d'Adda in the diocese of Milan deserves mention if only for its four ancient paintings of the saint which are important for a study of his iconography.

The saint's remains were solemnly translated to Pavia in 930 and spent more time in the Basilica of St Michael there before their return to Bobbio. As a result of these events Pavia formerly had two churches dedicated to the Irishman. One has now disappeared; the other building, no longer used as a church, is still an interesting specimen of Lombardic architecture and stands in the Via San Colombano.

About eleven other parish churches in Lombardy are dedicated to the Irish saint – two in the diocese of Bobbio, three in Tortona, two in Bergamo and one each in Como, Brescia and Bormio. One of the peaks overlooking the Valtellina, the Vietnam of the early seventeenth century, is the Corno di San Colombano, rising to a height of over nine thousand feet and with a chapel dedicated to the saint on its slopes.

Piacenza

Bobbio and its neighbourhood have already been sufficiently treated of. The province of Piacenza has four other parishes dedicated to St Columban and the city of Reggio Emilia has a fifth, in its south-eastern suburbs.

A very ancient Church of St Columban is still standing on the Via Parigi in the city of Bologna. It may date back as early as the seventh century and though often suppressed and no longer a parish church, it is still used by a confraternity for religious services. It is said to have formerly possessed the first campanile built in this city of towers.

Veronese

The Abbey of Bobbio once owned large estates in the vicinity of Lake Garda but a number of churches dedicated to the Irishman in this region seem to have disappeared.

Not far from Rovereto, between the Lake and Trent, the Ponte di San Colombano lies across a deep ravine, with an ancient shrine of the saint dangerously poised on the cliff beside it.

One parish in the province of Treviso is dedicated to the saint, and a locality known as Colombano will be found in the province of Rovigo.

Tuscany

Two parish churches in the diocese of Florence, one about six miles west of the city and the other about twelve miles south, are dedicated to the Irishman. The city of Lucca had a St Columban's Church as early as the eighth century, with a hospice attached to it which provided board and lodgings for the poor. Church and hospice are now gone, but I noticed when viewing the well-preserved city walls that the bastion which now stands near the site of the former church and hospice is still called the Baluardo San Colombano.

St Fridian, Lucca's Irish patron, is credited with having changed the course of the River Serchio which flows through the city, and further up the river is the village of San Colombano, with a parish church built about the eleventh century dedicated to the saint. He also figures, jointly or by himself, in the dedications of three parishes in the neighbouring diocese of Pontremoli.

III.

WORLDWIDE EXPANSION

So far we have dealt with the cult of St Columban in those countries on the European mainland where his own monastic work was carried out. It is a cult which stretches back over the centuries, in some cases almost to the era of Columban himself. But the great missionary effort of the Irish Church during the twentieth century has made the Irish people as a whole, both clergy and laity, once more aware of the work of the early Irish missionaries. As a result Columban has been made the patron saint of several Irish ecclesiastical movements and his name has been brought by Irish missionaries to the farthest ends of the earth.

In 1916 the idea of St Columban's Foreign Mission Society (for years known in Ireland as the Maynooth Mission to China) was born and the first Columban missionaries began to work in Hanyang in central China in 1920. Through the work of the Columban Fathers the saint's name was soon being given to parishes and churches in new countries and new continents. For instance, the first parish staffed by Columban Fathers in Shanghai became St Columban's parish; the college of the new society in Rome was naturally baptised the Collegio Missionario di San Colombano. Since its beginning the society has carried St Columban's name and patronage not only to China, but also to Japan, Korea, Burma, the Philippines, USA, Australia, New Zealand and to several of the South American countries.

It has even added Columban's name to the toponymy of the New World, for the United States government established a new postal address, St Columbans, to designate the spot where the United States headquarters of the society is situated.

In 1922 the Missionary Sisters of St Columban were established, the first Irish sisterhood to be set up specifically for work on the foreign missions. Four years later the first group of Columban Sisters sailed from Ireland to China. In 1922 the Knights of St Columban appeared on the scene in Ireland for the express purpose of countering discrimination against Catholics.

Columban's name did not become linked with an ecumenical enterprise for another sixty years. On 23 November 1983 the Columbanus Community of Reconciliation, founded by Fr Michael Hurley, SJ, was set up in Belfast. This is a residential community of Protestants and Catholics who bear witness to their common Christianity by their joint prayer, crossing of religious barriers and mutual respect for different Christian traditions. From being the forgotten exile, Columban had made a great come-back, and various groups of his fellow-countrymen were proud to affix his name to their banner.

The worldwide dissemination of his name and fame has continued undimmed during the past number of years. In 1950 an altar dedicated to him was erected in the crypt of St Peter's, Rome. At Lourdes the Secours Catholique has named a hostel for pilgrims in his honour. Finally, as if to set the seal on his crossing of national boundaries, his feast was added to the general calendar of the Church in 1969 and may now be celebrated liturgically throughout the world wherever the Roman rite is followed.

EPILOGUE

What others thought

The old Irish custom of each passer-by adding a stone to the chieftain's cairn as a mark of esteem (*cloch a chur ar a leacht*) has had its parallel in Columban's case in the great number of distinguished personages down the centuries who have paid tribute to his work. From Pope Sylvester II at the end of the first millennium to Pope John Paul II at the end of the second, the popes have been lavish in their praise of his achievements, while scholars, writers and statesmen have all placed their bouquets on his tomb. Of the many interesting comments which have been make on his work, space permits the inclusion here of only a handful of those stones which had been added to his cairn during the past century or so.

One of the most illustrious of those who have laboured under the impulse of Christianity for the fusion of the two greatest races of the West.
Montalembert

St Columban is the saint of the bibliophiles.
Gabriele D'Annunzio

The Celtic missionary genius had produced individuals of outstanding energy, it had given the world magnificent

apostolic personalities. Of these Columban was probably the greatest.
Georges Goyau

St Benedict did not reach manhood until the day he came to dwell in the house of St Columban.
Dom Cabrol

The more light that is shed by scholars on the period known as the Middle Ages, the clearer it becomes that it was thanks to the initiative and labours of Columban that the rebirth of Christian virtue and civilisation over a great part of Gaul, Germany and Italy took place.
Pope Pius XI

Columban is a new Moses but a Moses humanised by the smile of St Francis.
Père Dandin, de l'Oratoire

May the great missionary Columban obtain from God that he will put back in the heart of those whom he converted a little of the evangelical spirit which Columban taught them.
Louis Madelin, famous French historian

We must await the coming of St Bernard to witness an ascendency comparable to his. St Columban is one of the very great men who have dwelt in this land of France. He is, with Charlemagne, the greatest figure of our Early Middle Ages.
Léon Cathlin, poet, novelist and dramatist (who wrote *La lumière des brebis* on Columban's monks)

If any man was ever endowed with the European spirit,
that man was surely St Columban.
André Billy de l'Académie Goncourt

St Columban is not only a great Irishman but one of the
greatest Europeans of his time.
Seán MacBride

St Columban was the zealous servant of the Papacy as
well as the propagator of monastic greatness. He gave
us at the same time the example of submission to the
supreme authority and of courage in the struggles for the
triumph of just causes.
Pope John XXII

A sort of prophet of Israel, brought back to life in
the sixth century, as blunt in his speech as Isaias or
Jeremias ... For almost fifty years souls were stirred by
the influence of St Columban. His passing through the
country started a real contagion of holiness.
Daniel-Rops, de l'Académie Française

St Columban is the patron saint of those who seek to
construct a united Europe.
Robert Schuman, French Minister for Foreign Affairs

St Columban's spirit still survives in his modern disciples
who go forth from Ireland to bring to the world the true
meaning of life and the blessings of Christian thought and
practice.
Eamon de Valera

Prayers to St Columban

Columban, beg the Lord
Not to abandon me,
Let me return to thee;
Columban, beg the Lord.

– a verse of the poem *Nocte dieque gemo quia sum peregrinus et egens,* composed by an Irish monk who had fled from Bobbio to evade chastisement and while teaching in Verona composed these verses seeking permission to return (c.850).

A Dhia, is éachtach mar a thug tú chun a chéile i mbeatha Cholumbáin bheannaithe díograis chun an soiscéal a chraoladh agus dícheall chun beatha an mhanaigh a chaitheamh. Tabhair dúinn, iarraimid ort, trína impí agus a shampla, tusa a lorg thar an uile ní agus ár ndícheall a dhéanamh chun líon na gcreidmheach a mhéadú. Sin é ár nguí chugat trí Chríost ár dTiarna.
– From *An Leabhar Aifrinn Rómhánach* (1973)

Further Reading

Lengthy bibliographies on St Columban and his writings will be found in J. Kenney, *The Sources for the Early History of Ireland* (New York, 1929) and in the books by Dubois and Walker listed below. These can now be supplemented by the bibliography in J. Strzelczyk, *Iroszkoci w Kulturze Sredniowiecznej Europy* (Warsaw, 1987), which includes articles and books which are rarely found in Ireland. There is no point, therefore, in repeating a long list of titles which is already accessible elsewhere, and nothing is required here except to provide the reader with some guidance for further study and to indicate a few additional titles which were published subsequent to the preparation of the bibliographies mentioned above.

1. Columban's writings

The Irish Penitentials, Dublin, 1963. L. Bieler (ed.) (contains the Latin text of Columban's Penitential, with an English translation and an introduction on Irish penitential literature).

Le Pénitentiel de Saint Columban, Tournai, 1958. J. Laporte (ed.) (contains the Latin text of same, with a French translation and a long discussion of the document).

Studies on the language and style of Columba the Younger (Columbanus), Amsterdam, 1971. J.W. Smit (textual criticism of passages from Letters I–V and from Sermon 1 and examination of the authorship of the poems).

Santci Columbani Opera, Dublin, 1957. G.S.M. Walker (ed.) (contains the Latin text of all Columban's writings, including some which are doubtfully attributed to him, and a literal translation into English).

'On the new edition of the Opera Sancti Columbani' by M. Esposito, in *Classica et Mediaevalia*, 21, 1960, pp. 184–203.

2. The Life of Columban by Jonas

'Vitae Columbani Abbatis discipulorumque eius libri duo' in *Monumenta Germaniae Historica, S.S. rer. Merov.*, iv (1902), pp. 1–152. B. Krusch (ed.)

Ionae Vitae Sanctorum Columbani etc. *(SS. rer. Ger. in usum scholarum)*, Hanover and Leipzig, 1905 (this is the best edition, with a scholarly introduction in Latin). B. Krusch (ed.)

Additional work by Krusch on the text of Jonas will be found in *MGH, SS. rer. Merov.*, vii, ii (1920), pp. 822–7.
Unfortunately very few Irish libraries possess the Krusch edition of Jonas, and the Latin text (less perfect) may be most easily accessible in Migne, *PL.*, Vol. 87, 1011–84.

'The manuscripts of the Vita S. Columbani' in *Trans. RIA*, xxxii, c (Dublin 1902–4), pp. 1–132, provides photographic reproductions of some of the most important MSS of Jonas and textual criticism of them. H.J. Lawlor

Vita Columbani et discipulorum eius, Piacenza, 1965. M. Tosi (ed.)

Vie de Saint Columban et de ses disciples (Bellefontaine, 1988). French translation of Jonas by A. de Vogüé.

3. Modern Lives of St Columban

P. Buzzi, *Columbano d'Irlanda, il santo ed il poeta*, Locchi, 1921

H. Concannon, *Life of Saint Columban*, Dublin, 1915

M.M. Dubois, *Un pionnier de la civilisation occidentale*: *Saint Columban*, Paris, 1950

M.M. Dubois, *Saint Columban, A Pioneer of Western Civilisation*, trans. J. O'Carroll, Dublin, 1961

J.J. Laux, *Der heilige Kolumban, sein Leben und seine Schriften*, Freiburg, 1919 (In German, for the most part a translation of Metlake)

E.J. MacCarthy, *St Columban*, Nebraska-New York, 1972 (Montalembert's account with much extra material)

F. MacManus, *Saint Columban*, Dublin-London, 1963

E. Martin, *St Colomban*, Paris, 1905 (3rd ed. 1921)

G. Metlake, *Life and Writings of St Columban*, Philadelphia, 1914

J. Roussel, *St Colomban et l'épopée colombanienne*, 2 vols, Bescançon, 1941/42

J. Wilson, *Life of St Columban*, Dublin, 1953

4. Special questions regarding St Columban's life

On the chronology of the saint, see 'The Chronology of St Columban', by J. O'Carroll, in *Ir. Theol. Quarterly*, January 1957, pp. 76–95. For an earlier controversy regarding the date of St Columban's birth, see A. Gwynn, 'The Date of St Columban's Birth', in *Studies*, September 1918, pp. 474–84 and June 1919, pp. 66–8 and reply by H. Concannon, id., pp. 59–66.

For other aspects of the saint's life and writings, the following should be consulted:

F. Blanke, *Columban und Gallus*, Zurich, 1940

M. Lapidge, 'The authorship of the Adonic verses "Ad Fidolium", attributed to Columbanus', in *Studi Medievali*, 3rd ser. 18, 1977, 2, pp. 249–314

H. Löwe 'Columbanus und Fidolius', in *Deutsches Archiv*, 37, 1981, pp. 1–19

E.J. MacCarthy, 'Portrait of S. Columban', in *Ir. Eccles. Rec.*, lxxiv, 1950, pp. 110–15

G. Mitchell, 'St Columbanus on Penance' in *Ir. Theol. Quarterly*, 1951, pp. 43–54

J.F. O'Doherty, 'St Columbanus and the Roman See', in *Ir. Eccles. Rec.*, xlii, 1933, pp. 1–10

A. Oennerfors, 'Die Latinität Columbas des Jüngeren in neuem Licht', in *Zeitschr. f. Kirchengesch*, 83, 1972, 1, pp. 52–60

D.D.C Pochin Mould, 'St Columban and the Mass', in *Ir. Eccles. Rec.*, xcvii, 1962, pp. 296–303

5. Cult and monasteries

Mélanges Colombaniens (Paris, 1951), a collection of the papers read at the International Congress at Luxeuil in 1950, is a treasure-house of information on this subject, besides containing useful articles on the saint's humanism (L. Bieler), his Penitential (G. Mitchell), his Irish training (A. Gwynn) and his relations with various parts of Western Europe. For the cult of St Columban in general, see L. Gougaud, *Gaelic Pioneers of Christianity* (transl. V. Collins), Dublin 1923, and *Les Saints irlandais hors l'Irlande*, Louvain-Oxford, 1936 and for the greater Columbanian monasteries, see T. Ó Fiaich, *Gaelscrínte san Eoraip*, Dublin 1986.

The relevant articles in *Columbanus and Merovingian Monasticism*, Oxford 1981 and *Die Iren und Europa*, Stuttgart, 1982 should also be consulted.

Each of the following contains more detailed information about the monastery or area mentioned in its title.

San Colombano e la sua opera in Italia (proceedings of historical congress held in Bobbio in September 1951) Bobbio, 1953

F. Cabrol, *Luxeuil et Saint Colomban*, Luxeuil, 1926

J.M. Clarke, *The Abbey of St Gall as a centre of literature and art*, Cambridge, 1926

C.B. Curti-Pasini, *Il culto di S. Colombano in San Colombano al Lambro*, Lodi, 1923.

A. Maestri, *Il culto di San Colombano in Italia*, Piacenza, 1955

M. Stokes, *Six months in the Apennines in search of vestiges of the Irish saints in Italy*, London, 1892 (for Bobbio and district)

M. Stokes, *Three Months in the Forests of France*, London, 1895 (for Luxeuil and district)

A. Tommasini, *Irish Saints in Italy*, London, 1937, (transl. from Italian by J.F. Scanlan)

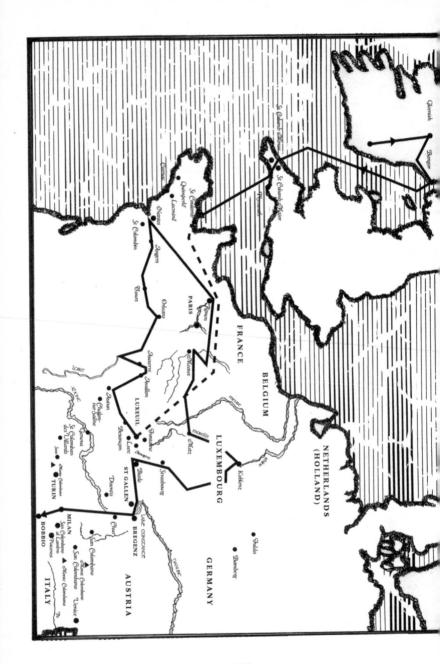